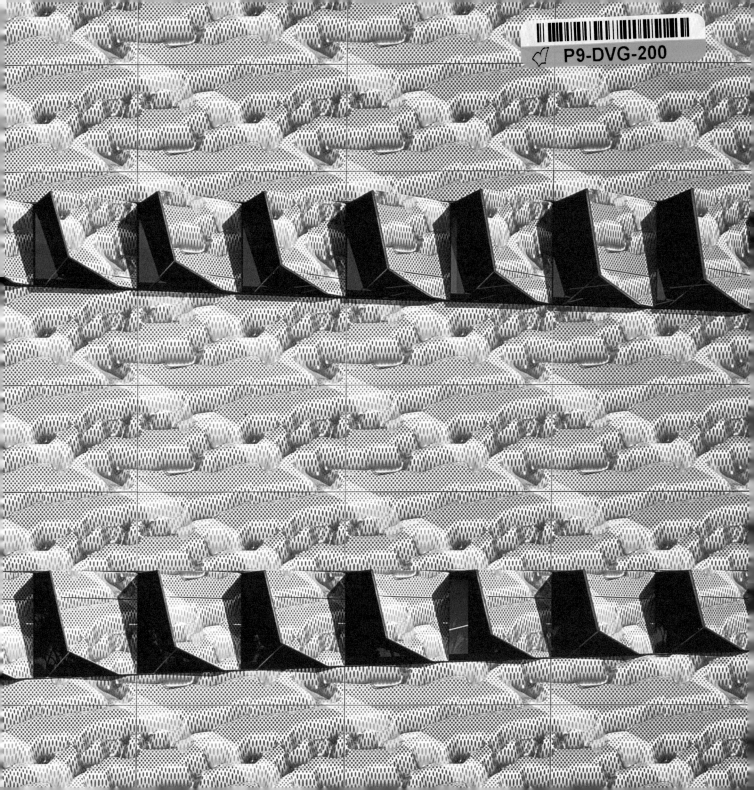

NEW DIRECTIONS IN AUSTRALIAN ARCHITECTURE

Philip Goad
Photography **Patrick Bingham-Hall**

PERIPLUS

CONTENTS

CONTENTS

D House. New Farm, Qld. 2001. Architect - Donovan Hill

Wardle House. Kew, Vic. 2000. Architect - John Wardle

*These new world projects are a feat of manipulation,
emendation and application. What they amount to is a
form of translation: of syntax, perspectives and images,
wrapped in the softest pessimistic dust.
The question they pose is, 'Do you love me'?*

*In the new world we are now dramatising our myths.
Half in love with this easeful land, we summon up illicit
visions of our ease. The honking chorus of native geese are
seen to rise and fly as swans. Not so this work.*

*These new world projects don the rubber gloves of
imagination and grasp the all-too-accommodating
orthodoxies of the old world. Time must have a stop.*

*In the new world, 'reality' may well be hauled in as just
another sham; we should have no truck with any positing
of the 'real'. But the 'here' and 'now' does matter.*

Peter Corrigan, Parts Unknown (1994)[1]

INTRODUCTION

Perceptions of the state of contemporary Australian architecture differ wildly. There is no clear picture. Nor should there be. Mythologised images of Australia are always partial in their truth and that is their attraction. The idea of a rude yet ineffably elegant shed/house set wistfully within a landscape paradise is what others would desire of Australian architecture. And such a phenomenon does exist in some parts of the country. However it is clearly not the case for much of urbanised Australia. Such a partial view obscures the richness and complexity of contemporary Australian architecture. One can make some generalisations and these, it must be said, are not necessarily peculiar to Australia. The local architecture culture is one dedicated to production. Theorising and design experiment does not emerge from within the academy or within the journals, but on the building site. Even the most intellectually sophisticated recent Australian architecture gains its credibility not through the pages of discourse, but through the building and actual testing of design propositions. In that respect, Australian architecture culture is traditionally conservative and suspicious of polemic, but only insofar as the notion of production is predicated on opportunity. One can build in Australia, and from a young age (generally) as an architect. Rather than invoke the hackneyed notion that Australia, as a postcolonial nation, is an apparently young culture and that we are moving through various stages of infancy and adolescence, the idea of youth should be applied to the culture generally. Its progressive practitioners are mostly young, and as a result, the veneration of architectural elders is practised lightly. Nor are design traditions sacred.

The common thread that links Australian architecture is an ethos of willing experiment. This is not an accusation of flippancy, or a lack of consistency in ideas. There is about contemporary Australian architecture, a freshness and an openness of brow that comes with the territory. It is indeed a continent relatively unsettled, underdeveloped, and poised at the edges of world cultures. Australia is neither quite East nor West, but it is undeniably part of Asia. It is a place that is in a simultaneous and constant state of, on the one hand, searching for identity and on the other, a proudly parochial defence of difference.

The aims of this book therefore, are not entirely new. A glimpse of contemporary Australian architecture from the past ten years is provided, but that glimpse is itself tantalisingly partial. Any overview is by necessity selective, and this is evidenced by publications in the past twenty years on contemporary Australian architecture.[2] This book is different, featuring the work of just fourteen architecture practices. Most are 'young' architecture firms with a recognisable body of built work that

[1] These quotations by Melbourne architect Peter Corrigan 1939- introduced a 1994 exhibition in Stuttgart on recent Melbourne architecture organised by NMBW, a group of Melbourne architects, Marika Neustupny, Nigel Bertram, Bindi McClean and Andrew Wilson. The lyricism of these lines still holds sway for characterising Australian architecture and I have taken the liberty of selecting for quotation four of an original six

of Corrigan's to introduce this essay. See *Parts Unknown*, catalogue to the Exhibition of Melbourne Architecture, Architektur-galerie am Weissenhof, Stuttgart, Germany, 3 November 1993 – 15 January 1994, NMBW, Melbourne, 1993, p1.
[2] The 1983 travelling exhibition *Old Continent, New Building: Contemporary Australian Architecture* was a catholic review of Australian architecture with written contributions

by Philip Cox, Leon Paroissien, Conrad Hamann, and Jennifer Taylor. See Leon Paroissien and Michael Griggs (eds), *Old Continent, New Building: Contemporary Australian Architecture*, Sydney: David Ell Press in association with the Design Arts' Committee of the Australia Council, 1983. In issue 4, 1984, *International Architect's* special issue on Australian architecture featured one work from each of twenty-one

signals achievement as well as potential. The choice has been deliberate in not focusing on Australian architects with high international profiles such as Harry Seidler, Glenn Murcutt, Philip Cox, Daryl Jackson, Edmond and Corrigan, and Denton Corker Marshall. Their influence and contribution to the development of late twentieth century Australian architecture is undeniable and ongoing. Instead, the firms featured in this book indicate the realisation of new directions in Australian architecture at the beginning of a new century.

Between 1968 and 1969, the New York publishing house George Braziller brought out the New Directions series and featured contemporary architecture in the United States, Great Britain, Italy, Germany, Japan, Switzerland, the Soviet Union, Africa and Latin America. The series gave a brief and fascinating insight to an architecture culture at a particular moment in time. Thirty years later, a similar series could be initiated on those smaller countries across the globe where architectural production is at its most intense and productive – Holland, Spain, Chile, Finland, and Australia. So in many respects this book is not an historical text, but a litmus test for the next decade of Australian architecture.

architecture firms and depicted a broad range of work across all states except Western Australia. Special issues on Australia compiled by the international magazines, *The Architectural Review* 1100, October 1988, *Casabella* 550, October 1988, *L'architecture d'aujourd'hui* 285, February 1993, and Denmark's *B* 52/53, 1995-1996, all attempted to engineer different images and different heroes for Australian architecture. Graham Jahn's *Contemporary Australian Architecture* Sydney: State Library New South Wales Press; Basel, Switzerland: G+B Arts International, 1994, followed a similar format while Andrew Metcalf's *Thinking Architecture: Theory in the Work of Australian Architects* Red Hill, ACT: Royal Australian Institute of Architects, 1995, profiled one work by each of twenty-eight architects with theoretical annotations. Most recently, Davina Jackson and Chris Johnson's *Australian Architecture Now* London: Thames & Hudson, 2000 avoided the highlighting of individual firms by an encyclopaedic focus on exemplars, types and tendencies.

AN ARCHIPELAGO OF ARCHITECTURE CULTURES

And her five cities, like five teeming sores,
Each drains her: a vast parasite robber state
Where second-hand Europeans pullulate
Timidly on the edge of alien shores.
AD Hope, Australia (1939)[3]

AD Hope's visceral description of the capital cities of each of the mainland Australian states as "five teeming sores" is confronting. It is an analogy for their irrevocable and wounding force on a giant continent that has only been settled since 1788. Unlike Europe, where successive cultures had overlaid layer after layer of urbanisation and agriculture upon the land, the introduction of 19th century settlement and modern industrialisation in Australia was rather more brutal, and especially so on a land tracked and lined by the lightness of its indigenous inhabitants.[4] The idea of a sore is a harsh judgment of colonial settlement given the occasional Picturesque intent of some of the nation's first surveyors. However, if sores they became, as scars they have remained - enduring and permanent . Indeed their growth has escalated ever since. Today, over 60% of Australia's population live in these capital cities, and with the exception of the nation's capital, Canberra, each of these cities is located on the coast, next to water: a river, the sea or a harbour. As an obverse to the Australian aboriginal population being connoted as 'fringe dwellers', architectural critic Philip Drew has categorised Australians as being a nation of 'coast

3 AD Hope, *Collected Poems*, 1930-1965, Sydney: Angus and Robertson, 1966.
4 For elaboration on this notion of lines and tracks across the Australian landscape, see Krim Benterrak, *Reading the country: introduction to nomadology*, Fremantle, WA: Fremantle Arts Centre Press, 1984; Paul Carter, *The road to Botany Bay: an essay in spatial history*, London: Faber and Faber, 1987; Bruce Chatwin; *The songlines*, London: Cape, 1987; David Tacey, *Edge of the Sacred: transformation in Australia*, Blackburn North, Vic: HarperCollins, 1995.

dwellers', always with an eye to the horizon above the sea and invariably attempting to defer from the harshness of the Australian interior landscape.[5] While there is much truth to his thesis, he overlooks the fact that each of the coastal cities has a circumference. Each city has experienced relatively uncontrolled radial growth, and twentieth century suburbia is a necessary symptom and corollary. Each Australian city is an island within a much larger landscape. It is as if Sydney, Melbourne, Brisbane, Perth, Adelaide, Hobart, and Darwin make up an archipelago of settlement with a myriad of smaller islands beyond.[6]

The analogy of urbanised Australia constituting an archipelago of conurbations can be taken further.[7] Given the vast scale of the Australian continent, each city is defined by a different climatic condition, a different landscape and topography, and often a different pattern of settlement as the colonial plans of the British contrasted with each location. The result is a variegated condition peculiar to other large New World countries such as the United States, Canada and Brazil. In cultural terms, diversity can also be identified. In architecture, each city possesses fundamentally different cultures of education, patronage, professional discourse, approaches to construction and materials, and building within the landscape.[8] Such a condition makes comparison across various Australian architectures tendentious, and the notion of a coherent Australian architecture impossible to pinpoint.

In the late 1880s and early 1890s, local architectural commentators such as John Sulman, James Green, E Wilson Dobbs, and others attempted to define an Australian style of architecture as a celebratory gesture to the one hundred years of European settlement since 1788.[9] Their efforts were in vain, and close analysis of their writings (which read as personal manifestos) indicates opinions that were essentially city-based, with the strongest opinions polarised between Sydney and Melbourne, the two most populous cities in the country. Little has changed. In the past ten years, building production and architectural discourse in Australia has been dominated by these two cities. Even so, the distant islands of the archipelago, especially Perth, Brisbane, and Darwin have revealed startling points of difference that celebrate alternative ways of building and thinking about architecture. Isolation and introspection as a phenomenon, even within the confines of Australia, has been productive. In many ways, the buildings that emanate from these less populous centres are salutary reminders of the essential heterogeneity of position within Australian architectural practice.

Each Australian city defers, often unconsciously, to its own architectural traditions and each city also responds in unpredictable ways to its new arrivals. Sometimes the work of recently arrived or émigré architects can act as a catalyst to shifts in the local position. Darwin is a perfect example. There, a combination of early twentieth century public servants' houses built in slatted timber with broad eaves

[5] Philip Drew, *The coast dwellers: Australians living on the edge*, Ringwood, Victoria: Penguin, 1994.
[6] These smaller islands are the Australian country and provincial towns of which centres like Canberra, Alice Springs, Launceston, Newcastle, Geelong, Kalgoorlie, Rockhampton, Cairns and Townsville must be considered the more important.
[7] I am grateful to Melbourne architect, artist and poet Alex Selenitsch for this notion of archipelago and Australia. Drawn from conversations with him, I have speculated on

applying this notion to that of architecture cultures within Australia.
[8] The idea of an archipelago of architecture cultures underlying the development of twentieth century Australian architecture is implicit in the structure of Jennifer Taylor's *Australian Architecture Since 1960*, Canberra, ACT: RAIA Education Division, 1986.
[9] John Sulman, "An Australian Style", *Australasian Builders and Contractors News (ABCN)*, 14.5.1887; "Verandahs and Loggie", *ABCN*, 21.5.1887; "Bricks, Stone and Terra Cotta", *ABCN*, 18.6.1887. For a detailed examination of the Sulman articles, see

John Phillips, "John Sulman and the Question of an 'Australian Style of Architecture'", *Fabrications*, 8 July 1997, pp.87-116. James Izett, "Australasian Architecture", *ABCN*, 4.1.1890. James Green, "An Australian Style of Architecture I", *ABCN*, 18.10.1890; *ABCN*, 25.10.1890; *ABCN*, 1.11.1890; *ABCN*, 15.11.1890. TA Sisley, "The Australian Home – Facts, Fancies and Fallacies", *The Building and Engineering Journal*, 20.12.1890. E Wilson Dobbs, "An Australian Style of Architecture", *The Building and Engineering Journal*, 21.2.1891.

and ventilating roofs, the late 1930s houses of Beni Burnett (1889-1955)[10], the presence of World War II steel-framed and corrugated iron structures, and a habit of building out of the back of a utility truck lies behind a very specific environmentally responsive design tradition. In response to Australia's tropical 'Top End' with its distinct 'wet' and 'dry' seasons, a way of building and making spaces in demanding climatic conditions has developed. It is this way of building to which the firm Troppo and others in Darwin have responded with inventive planning and a shrewd understanding of local construction practices. Troppo's twenty years of practice[11] in Darwin has developed its own tradition, from which new work like the Rozak House in the savannah landscape outside Darwin represents the next step in consolidating that city's now distinctive contemporary architecture.

Burnett House. Darwin, NT. 1942.
Architect - Beni Burnett

Such a culture of approaching architecture is quite different from that in Sydney, Australia's oldest city. The weight of authorised taste and the legacy of the Colonial Georgian style has fostered urban and typological continuity through the formal stuccoed walls of Leslie Wilkinson, Hardy Wilson and John Moore[12], and more recently in the work of Espie Dods and Alex Tzannes. The teaching programs of The University of Sydney fostered this veneration of propriety and gentility for the first half of the twentieth century, and its influence still resonates through Sydney practice. However, this is not the only Sydney tradition. There is also reverence for the stylistic pedigree. This is evidenced by, on the one hand, the fifty year staunchly Modernist career of Harvard-educated Harry Seidler[13] and on the other, the organic tradition that blossomed in late 1950s Sydney.[14] Other traditions have prevailed, inspired by the no-nonsense Modernism of Sydney Ancher's Japanese-inspired later works, and Bill and Ruth Lucas' postwar experimental houses using exposed materials with unadorned structure. Ken Woolley's dual interest in the formal dexterity of Alvar Aalto's skillion roofs and internalised volumetric landscapes, and in the urbane surfaces of Italian Neoliberty architects' work of the late 1950s remains influential.

Mapleton House. Mapleton, Qld. 1991.
Architect - Richard Leplastrier

The greatest reverence, and justifiably so, is reserved for the tectonic and structural clarity, landscape appositeness, and the tragic-heroic presence in Sydney between 1957 and 1966 of Danish architect Jørn Utzon and his incomplete masterpiece, the Sydney Opera House (1957-73). Utzon's globally understood design methods have become touchstones of technique in Sydney. Practitioners like Glenn Murcutt[15] and Richard Leplastrier[16] have produced seminal non-urban works, mainly houses, that posit emphatic dialogues with the landscape and celebrate fundamental notions of prospect and refuge[17], and as

[10] David Bridgman, "Shadows and Space: The Domestic Architecture of Beni Burnett", B, 52/53, 1995-1996, pp18-25.
[11] Philip Goad, Troppo: architecture for the Top End, Sydney: Pesaro Publishing, 1999.
[12] Conrad Hamann, "Paths of Beauty: The Afterlife of Australian Colonial Architecture, Part I", Transition, 26, pp27-44. See also Philip Cox and Clive Lucas, "The Colonial Revival", Australian Colonial Architecture, Melbourne: Lansdowne Editions, 1978, pp227-255.
[13] The Graduate School of Design at Harvard University was a virtual East Coast Bauhaus in the 1940s when Seidler took his master class there with Professor Walter Gropius, founder of the original Weimar Bauhaus. After graduation in 1946, Seidler took the design course at Black Mountain College, North Carolina under another former Bauhaus

academic, Josef Albers. In 1947 he worked in New York for Marcel Breuer, another Bauhaus student and teacher. Historical documentation on the career of Harry Seidler is extensive. See Harry Seidler, Houses, Interiors and Projects, Sydney: Associated General Publishers, 1954; Peter Blake, Architecture for the New World: the work of Harry Seidler, Sydney: Horwitz, 1973; Kenneth Frampton, Philip Drew, Harry Seidler: four decades of architecture, London: Thames and Hudson, 1992; and Harry Seidler, Harry Seidler: selected and current works, Mulgrave, Vic.: Images Publishing Craftsman House, 1997; Alice Spigelman, Almost Full Circle: Harry Seidler, Sydney: Brandl and Schlesinger, 2001.
[14] This organic tradition, mainly Wrightian in origin, can be seen in the early work of Peter Muller. See Jacqueline Urford, The architecture of Peter Muller, MArch., University of Sydney, Sydney, 1995. Others who contributed to this tradition included: Bruce Rickard, Ian McKay, and the firm of Robertson and Hindmarsh. Others who can be linked to this organic tradition like Neville Gruzman were not only influenced by Wright's work but also

that of Mies van der Rohe and the principles of Japanese architecture. Gruzman's work, for example, represents a resolution of these diverse influences and their application to the Sydney landscape to achieve unique results.
[15] Philip Drew, Leaves of Iron: Glenn Murcutt, pioneer of an Australian architectural form, Sydney: Law Book Co., 1985; EM Farrelly, Three houses, Glenn Murcutt, London: Phaidon, 1993; Francoise Fromonot, Glenn Murcutt: works and projects, London: Thames and Hudson, 1995.
[16] Rory Spence, Sources of theory and practice in the work of Richard Leplastrier, MArch, University of New South Wales, Sydney, 1997.
[17] In The Experience of Landscape (New York: John Wiley and Sons, 1975), Jay Appleton proposed, and argued a new theoretical approach to landscape aesthetics, including 'habitat theory' and 'prospect-refuge theory' based on an analysis of research literature and experience in a wide area of art and science.

pieces of architecture, these works appear unassailable in their dedication to the making of architecture. Internationally, it is Murcutt's rigorous typological explorations of the linear house that have had the greatest impact. Winner of the Alvar Aalto Medal in 1992, Murcutt has continued in each finely detailed house to pursue the Modernist project for an ideal villa. His houses, with their ability

Done House. Balmoral, NSW. 1992.
Architect - Glenn Murcutt

to be spatially both open and closed, are an intriguing condensation of fundamental architectural concerns. He is best known for houses outside Sydney, in startlingly beautiful rural or bush sites. So what is his relationship to Sydney's architecture culture? It is true that that his

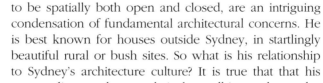

Carruthers House. Mt Irvine, NSW. 1980.
Architect - Glenn Murcutt

metropolitan works are relatively small in number and arguably less public than his remote works. Yet they are equally revealing. His Littlemore House is an urban sliver in 19th century Woollahra (1986), and the Done House, Balmoral (1992), presents a formal Miesian box to the streets with dreamy Mediterranean courtyards within. These houses demonstrate different concerns such as an interest in the work of Pierre Chareau and Antonio Coderch de Sentmenat. More importantly, they indicate Murcutt's ability to adapt to Sydney's urban context, not just its fabled sites of natural beauty.

In many ways, the buildings by Utzon, Murcutt, and Leplastrier echoed the phenomenological design teaching that characterised Sydney's various architectural schools from the 1960s to the 1990s. The influence of architect-academics like George Molnar, Peter Kollar, and Adrian Snodgrass, as well as the teaching on construction, landscape and architectural history by Myles Dunphy (1891-1985), and the painter Lloyd Rees (1895-1988), seemed to coalesce in these architects' works.[18] Given such a context, the work of Tonkin Zulaikha Greer, Stutchbury and Pape, and Engelen Moore needs to be viewed as working within or counter to that Sydney context, its tradition of object lessons and time-honoured Modernist pedigree, and its habits of measured urbanity and harnessing the private landscape view.

In Brisbane, a benign sub-tropical climate has allowed an architecture that dissolves spatial boundaries, and determines its course from climate and the controlled entry of sunlight. At the same time, the traditions of the elevated Queensland house have not gone unnoticed. Since the 1970s, the houses of Russell Hall, Rex Addison, and Lindsay and Kerry Clare have epitomised the close knowledge of timber construction, and the formal and expressive qualities

Hall House. Wilston, Qld. 1985.
Architect - Russell Hall

[18] George Molnar, Lloyd Rees, and Adrian Snodgrass taught at the University of Sydney. Peter Kollar taught at the University of New South Wales. Myles Dunphy taught at the Sydney Technical College. For notes on Snodgrass, Dunphy and Rees, see Jennifer Taylor, *Australian Architecture Since 1960*, Canberra, ACT: RAIA Education Division, 1986, 1990, pp15-16, 35-36, 43. Myles Dunphy's son Milo was also an important Sydney environmentalist. See Peter Meredith, *Myles and Milo*, St Leonards, NSW: Allen & Unwin, 1999.

of the corrugated iron roof.[19] They realise Melbourne architect Nahum Barnet's call a century before for a "Climatic Architecture."[20] Their houses also acknowledge early 20th century Brisbane architect Robin Dods' emphasis on the importance of craft and the scaling of space for the individual.[21] The serene spaces of Dods' verandahs find a different reflection in the inside/outside linearity of Brit Andresen and Peter O'Gorman's houses. By contrast, an interloper to Brisbane can inject different notions of what architecture might mean in Queensland. The presence in Brisbane of James Birrell (1928-) since the late 1950s brought mass in the form of robustly jointed, boldly modelled and imprinted brick and concrete structures like the Wickham Terrace Car Park, Brisbane (1958-61), and Hartley Teakle Building at the University of Queensland (1966-69).[22] Brian Donovan and Timothy Hill have capitalised on Birrell's hybrid and idiosyncratic monumentality. Their work constantly crosses between the opposites of mass and lightness, open and closed form. In their hands, a new tradition is made possible for Brisbane.

Tamrookum Chapel. Tamrookum, Qld.
1915. Architect - Robin Dods

Addison Studio. Taringa, Qld. 1998.
Architect - Rex Addison

Broadway Showroom. Nedlands, WA.
1964. Architect - Julius Elischer

Across the other side of the continent in Perth, the capital of Western Australia, climatic and geographic conditions shift again. Sand, a piercing summer sun and a dryness that is relieved on a daily basis by the 'Fremantle Doctor', the regular cooling wind from the Indian Ocean, are initial determinants for a local architecture culture. It is an architecture culture that has oscillated between two poles. There has been Mediterranean comparison in the Romanesque Revival of Rodney Alsop and Conrad Sayce's Winthrop Hall at the University of Western Australia (1931), Marshall Clifton's low-key Spanish-inspired houses of the 1930s[23], and RJ (Gus) Ferguson's (in association with Professor Gordon Stephenson) university-building palette of spreading gable roofs and reinforced concrete frame and infills. In equal strength there has been an opposing interest in the clear lessons of an austere scientifically based Modernism and the seemingly contradictory ideas of the elaborated surface of the postwar wall. Of this latter path, the inverted

Learmonth International Airport.
Exmouth, WA. 2000.
Architect - Jones Coulter Young

[19] *Australian architects: Rex Addison, Linsday Clare and Russell Hall,* Manuka, ACT: RAIA Education Division, 1990; Peter Hyatt, *Local heroes: architects of Australia's Sunshine Coast,* North Ryde, NSW: Craftsman House, 2000.
[20] Nahum Barnet, "Climatic Architecture", *Victorian Review,* 1.11.1882.
[21] For a very early account of the work of Robin Dods, see John Sydney Egan, The work of Robin Dods, ARIBA, Sydney: BArch, University of Sydney, 1932. See also Neville H Lund,

"Robin Dods", in Howard Tanner (ed.), *Architects of Australia,* South Melbourne: Macmillan, 1981, pp86-95; Robert Riddell, "RS Dods: Towards an Australian Architecture, 'Rightness' – A Design Etiquette", in J. Willis, P. Goad and A. Hutson, *FIRM(ness) commodity DE-light?: questioning the canons, Papers from the Sixteenth Annual Conference of the Society of Architectural Historians, Australia and New Zealand,* Melbourne, 1998, pp295-300; and Robert Riddell, "The houses of RS Dods", in R. Blythe and R. Spence (eds.), *Thresholds:*

Papers of the Sixteenth Annual Conference of the Society of Architectural Historians, Australia and New Zealand, Launceston and Hobart, 1999, pp281-286.
[22] Andrew Wilson and John Macarthur (eds), *Birrell: work from the office of James Birrell,* Melbourne, Vic.: NMBW Publications, 1997.
[23] Barbara Chapman and Duncan Richards, *Marshall Clifton, architect and artist,* Fremantle, WA: Fremantle Arts Centre Press, 1989.

T-shaped sunscreens of Howlett and Bailey's Council House, Perth (1963), the deep abstract window reveals of Julius Elischer's Broadway Showroom, Nedlands, Perth (1964), and the encrusted blockwork façade of Iwan Iwanoff's Dianella Heights House, Perth (1977), seem to foreshadow one aspect of Jones Coulter Young's repertoire of university buildings. The conscientious scientism of their construction and the responsible control of shade are offset by wilfully figurative flourishes. Just like the distinctly unusual shapes and vibrant colours that one finds in indigenous flora in Western Australia, these are startling apparitions. Jones Coulter Young's airport at Exmouth in remote Western Australia is totally unexpected, but in the scheme of Western Australia's architecture culture, it strikes a locally familiar chord.

Roma Mitchell Performing Arts Centre, Adelaide, SA. 2001.
Architect - Hassell

Roma Mitchell Performing Arts Centre, interior

Wright House, Springfield, SA. 1952.
Architect - Russell Ellis

In Adelaide, a certain austerity prevails in its architecture. The purity of Colonel Light's 1837 grid plan with its series of squares and broad streets, the graciousness of North Terrace, and Adelaide's touristic label as the 'city of churches' which boasts the great English architect William Butterfield's largest complete work, St. Peter's Cathedral, North Adelaide (1869-1904), imply a metropolis of great potential. However the infilling of Light's ideal plan has not been completed. There seems thus more space than necessary in Adelaide. The dryness of the climate and its intense Summer heat is relieved only by escape to the Adelaide Hills, the city's nearby 'Simla.' There are copious amounts of stone and brick, and the city's 1920s bungalows emphasise that sense of mass with their vast roofs and deep shaded porches. Model planning can be found in Adelaide's two best known garden suburbs, Colonel Light Gardens (1921), and the 'new town' of the 1950s, Elizabeth.[24] These are sober developments, unparalleled in the realisation of their idealism in Australia.[25] They contrast dramatically with compositional gems like Russell Ellis's Wright House, Springfield, Adelaide (1952), a curious combination of abstract cubes, a deeply perforated egg-crate screen and a framed door with porthole windows set within leafy suburbia. The early works of Jack McConnell are carefully studied examples of late 1930s Functionalist design that are unobtrusive, responsible, and sparely elegant. McConnell's name was once part of Hassell, the architecture firm that now has offices all over Australia. Even in one of Hassell's recent Adelaide buildings, the Roma Mitchell Centre for Performing Arts (2001), the palette is carefully subdued - red brick, with discreet glazed protrusions and a calmly non-emphatic mass. Adelaide's quietly consistent architecture culture is consolidated yet again.

[24] Robert Freestone, *Model Communities: the garden city movement in Australia*, Melbourne: Nelson, 1989. [25] Stephen Hamnett and Robert Freestone (eds.), *The Australian Metropolis: A Planning History*, St Leonards, NSW: Allen and Unwin, 2000.

Labassa. Caulfield, Vic. 1891.
Architect - JAB Koch

Gottlieb House. Caulfield, Vic. 1994.
Architect - Wood Marsh

As for Melbourne, climate and landscape seem to have no part in that culture's pact with obsessive artifice and formal experiment. It is a city that has its own internal archipelago of architecture cultures. Located in Australia's temperate south, relatively flat and with no obviously pressing need to respond solely to climate, Melbourne's architecture culture revels in discourse and meaning, in oppositions that are formal, political, social and spatial. Ever since the heyday of the 1880s when the so-called and historically maligned Boom Style was an intensely complex overlaying of classical screens and vigorous sculptural detail,[26] Melbourne architects have opted for exploring the surface as a rich canvas for representation, and the isolated architectural object as a testing ground for bold formal gestures. The sheer flamboyance of JA Koch's Labassa in suburban Caulfield (1891), a vast grey stucco villa, is matched by Wood Marsh's Gottlieb House (1994), also in Caulfield with a startling elliptical entry volume at the street and astonishing pebble-walls behind. Yet there are a myriad of other cultures simultaneously at work in Melbourne. The crafted compositions in timber of John Wardle and Sean Godsell are in complete contrast with Lyons' graphics-grappling projects on their unforgiving outer suburban sites. The tension evident in the different philosophies of design emanating from these practices and those of Kerstin Thompson, Ashton Raggatt McDougall, and Nation Fender Katsalidis constantly exacerbates and fosters debate within that city.

Some of these Australian 'islands' of architecture culture reveal more than others. They are infinitely more complex than these brief descriptions allow. Hobart and Launceston in Tasmania, the island state lying south of Australia's mainland, and Canberra, the nation's capital, also have their distinctive architecture cultures.[27] The significance and importance here is the sense of partial containment, and the almost hermetic nature of these local cultures, that make a demonstration of Australian architecture so nuanced and at times insular, and thus its current pluralism of position so remarkable. If the image of Australia's urbanised centres as teeming sores is unpalatable, it is because it is true. Each archipelago gains its economic and political sustenance from these cities, and this is in complete contradistinction to the humility of its indigenous inhabitants. Settlement has not been kind to the land, but two centuries later it continues to be an unalterable fact.

[26] Peter Kohane, "Classicism transformed: a study of façade composition in Victoria, 1885-1892", *Transition*, 10, pp27-36; George Tibbits, "Marvellous Melbourne", in Philip Goad, *A Guide to Melbourne Architecture*, Sydney: Watermark Press, 1999, pp54-57. [27] In Tasmania, for example, the experimental steel and glass houses of Esmond Dorney in the 1950s, the austere Anglo-Brutalism of Bush Parkes Shugg and Moon in the 1960s, and the clear Modern forms of Heffernan Nation and Viney in the 1970s laid the groundwork for a current generation of Tasmanian practitioners like Ken Latona, Leigh Woolley and Craig Rosevear. While clearly there are more practitioners that one might note, the critical observation to make is that a recognisably local idiom has persisted and continues to do so in Tasmania. For some historical data, see Jennifer Taylor, "Architecture in Tasmania from 1930 to 1980", *Transition*, 6, pp37-42.

CENTRE AND PERIPHERY

In the 1960s, a phrase came into vogue to describe Australia's embarrassment at its cultural and physical isolation, and its apparent backwardness and tardiness in keeping up to date with global fashion and events. It was the 'cultural cringe' – an inferiority complex of monumental proportions. The inference was that somehow Australia did not measure up to overseas standards. One of Australia's chief postwar cultural critics, the architect Robin Boyd (1919-71), was ironically occasionally guilty of the 'cringe'. While his contribution to the definition of a modern Australian architecture was immense[28], his later writings became increasingly self-deprecating.[29] Boyd's targets of vilification were almost always the visual state of the average Australian house, and the visual pollution and the technological primitivism of the Australian city. The Australian suburb was cast as the villain. From the mid-1970s onwards however, general perceptions within the architecture profession shifted dramatically as theories of inclusivism and regionalism were explored. The ordinary and the ugly of the suburbs were rediscovered as a possible source of formal inspiration and cultural redemption.

The turn to the suburbs was partly a reaction by a younger generation of architects to the focus in the late 1960s and 1970s on the monumental building program in Canberra. The nation's capital was a commissioning paradise for mature practices where bureaucracy appeared to dictate subdued aesthetic responses. But it was also there that the internationally known figures of John Andrews and Harry Seidler flexed their muscles in megastructural projects[30] while following the National Capital

[28] Boyd's major works of architectural history/commentary include: *Victorian Modern*, Melbourne: Victorian Architecture Students Society, 1947; *Australia's Home*, Melbourne, Melbourne University Press, 1952; *The Australian Ugliness*, Melbourne, FW Cheshire, 1960; and *The Puzzle of Architecture*, Melbourne: Melbourne University Press, 1965. For an extensive bibliography of Boyd's writings and introduction to his written oeuvre, see Philip Goad, "Pamphlets at the Frontier: Robin Boyd and the will to incite an Australian architectural culture", pp10-15, and the bibliography compiled by Goad in K Burns and H

Edquist (eds.), *Robin Boyd: the architect as critic*, Melbourne: Transition Publishing, 1989. On Boyd's life and work, see Geoffrey Serle, *Robin Boyd: a life*, Melbourne, Melbourne University Press, 1995, and the special issue on Robin Boyd, *Transition*, 38, 1992.
[29] This is especially evident in Robin Boyd, *The Great Great Australian Dream*, Sydney: Pergamon Press, 1972. For further analysis of the character of Boyd's writings, see Conrad and Chris Hamann, "Anger and The New Order: Some Aspects of Robin Boyd's Career", *Transition*, 2: 3/4, September/December 1981, p26-39.

[30] For example, Harry Seidler's Trade Group (Edmund Barton) Offices, Canberra 1970-74 and John Andrews International's Woden Offices Project, Woden, Canberra 1973 and Cameron Offices, Belconnen, Canberra (1976). For more on Andrews' work, see Jennifer Taylor, *John Andrews: architecture a performing art*, Melbourne: Oxford University Press, 1982.

Development Commission guidelines for the creation of a "white" Antipodean Washington DC in Late Modern style. The High Court of Australia (1980), and the National Gallery of Australia (1982), by Edwards Madigan Torzillo and Briggs, were two vast sculptural monoliths in concrete and glass that echoed in their siting the spatial field of Chandigarh, yet in their vigorous massing avoided the precision of IM Pei's East Building of the National Gallery of Art in Washington DC (1971-78). There was in these two buildings, a sense of isolation. Their appearance confirmed Canberra in the 1970s as neither 'city as centre' nor 'capital as bush'. Lost in space, they awaited more buildings to join them. They were temporarily located in that very peripheral state that some Australian architects were soon to find intriguing, but it was not Canberra that would be their focus.

The periphery was not the unpopulated bush or rural heartland of Australia, but the apparent cultural no-man's land of the sprawling middle and outer suburbs of the Australian city. It must be said that the suburbs had never been entirely neglected by architects, especially during the project house boom of the late 1960s.[31] Yet it was Peter Corrigan's missive from the United States in 1972[32] that broadcast the work of the Venturis, and his subsequent return to Australia in 1974[33] that sparked the latent aesthetic interest in the suburbs. Edmond and Corrigan's work added a polemical challenge to Hugh Stretton's environmental socio-political defence of the suburb as intrinsic to Australian way of life that had appeared in his landmark book, 'Ideas for Australian Cities' (1970).[34] That there could be an acknowledgment of and intellectual questioning of the aesthetics of the periphery was radical. By the late 1980s and early 1990s, the discussion had reached a new and self-consciously self-reflexive level of sophistication, especially through the writings of Melbourne architects Howard Raggatt and Ian McDougall[35], and also in Paul Morgan's research in the one-off issue of '38 South'.[36]

There was much less interest in the other Australian capital cities, where the Melbourne buildings of architects like Edmond and Corrigan were treated with either antagonism or polite disdain. In Melbourne, the periphery became a topic for discussion and the suburb enjoyed a new status as Australia's very own *terrain vague*. Here was the space that Spanish critic Ignasi Sola-Morales Rubio later described as "internal to the city, yet external to its everyday use".[37] In Europe, disused former industrial sites close to the city centre and with embodied potential qualified for such a term. In Australia, it was the suburbs, considered by the conservative sector of the profession as possessing no inherent virtues, either aesthetic or cultural, which were now sites of potential. A series of controversial churches and schools by Edmond and Corrigan in the 1980s[38] were the springboard for a new brand of polemic to be developed by a younger generation. Yet, for the most part, in every other capital city in Australia, such a discussion was rarefied and not to be had. The suburban

[31] For published material on 1960s and 1970s project houses, see Ian McKay et al, *Living & partly living: housing in Australia*, Melbourne: Thomas Nelson (Australia), 1971; Howard Tanner, *Australian housing in the seventies*, Sydney: Ure Smith, 1976; Jennifer Taylor, *Australian Architecture Since 1960*, Canberra, ACT: RAIA Education Division, (1986) 1990, pp141-163.
[32] Peter Corrigan, "Reflections on a new North American architecture: the Venturis", *Architecture in Australia*, 61, 1, February 1972, pp55-67.
[33] Conrad Hamann, *Cities of Hope: Australian Architecture and Design by Edmond and Corrigan 1962-92*, Melbourne: Oxford University Press, 1993, pp37-39.

[34] Hugh Stretton, *Ideas for Australian Cities*, Melbourne: Georgian House, 1970 (first published by the author also in 1970).
[35] For example, Ian McDougall, "Dispersion and the Encyclopaedic: Towards New Techniques for the City", *Backlogue: Journal of the Half Time Club*, 1, March 1992, pp34-41; and also "5 Projects: Ashton Raggatt McDougall", *Backlogue: Journal of the Half Time Club*, 1, March 1992, pp154-185. In the same journal, Shane Murray's article "Three Consequences for a Centralist Obsession", pp42-45 complements these views on the Australian city. See also *Fin de Siecle?: And the 21st Century*, Melbourne: RMIT, 1993; Leon van Schaik (ed.), *Transfiguring the ordinary*, Melbourne: Printed Books, 1995.

[36] *38 south: the graduate journal of architecture and urban design from RMIT*, Melbourne: Department of Architecture, Faculty of the Constructed Environment, RMIT, 1991.
[37] Ignasi Sola-Morales Rubio, "Terrain vague", in Cynthia C Davidson (ed.), *Anyplace*, London: MIT Press, 1995.
[38] For example, Resurrection Church and School, Keysborough, Victoria 1976-81; Chapel of St Joseph, Box Hill, Victoria 1976-78; St Francis Xavier Primary School, Frankston, Victoria (1984).

periphery was neglected and in many cases for very good reason. It was simply a matter of survival, there was literally no business there.

The neglect of the suburbs was in contrast to a heightened professional awareness of centre, of practice within the central city and its immediate environs. The 1990s saw the completion of major private and public projects of urban planning, projects of urban renewal, and urban insertion in the downtown and inner city areas that had been envisioned in the 1980s or earlier. Large scale urban redevelopment projects tended to centre on water: the revival of former industrial harbour land, and dockyards; or the refocusing of a city on a river or waterway. It was as if water was to be an urban panacea, that its allure as a real estate vista and as a setting for a retail promenade could ensure its future as a magnet for urbanity and peopled spaces. No Australian city was more self-conscious in its focus on centre and 'metropolitan improvement' in the 1990s than Sydney.

The prospect of the 2000 Olympic Games fuelled a desire to recover Sydney after the ravaging that the central city had experienced in the 1960s and 1970s. There was a need to physically reknit the city at all levels, as well as psychologically refocus Sydney in the mind of its people and its visitors. No less than 7 books on urban Sydney were published in 1999 and 2000.[39] While the corporate towers of Harry Seidler, Denton Corker Marshall, and others had added distinction to Sydney's skyline in the 1990s, their presence was not enough. Part of the process was driven by the need to introduce a bipolar view of Sydney during the Games when the Harbour and Homebush Bay were to form visitors' conceptions of the city.[40] This meant recouping the city's underlying infrastructure of transport, its streets and its public spaces. Hassell's Olympic Park Railway Station (1998), was designed as a pivotal public transport hub at the Homebush Bay Olympic site. Conceived by

Olympic Park Railway Station.
Homebush Bay, NSW. 1998. Architect - Hassell

its designers Ken Maher and Rodney Uren as 'below ground' rather than 'underground', it was intended that passengers alight in an airy open volume, almost as if the 'solid base' of the urban square outside had been folded down 6.5 metres to form a sunken space of public assembly. Above, a gracefully curving and concertina-like canopy - forming an organic analogy of a leaf floating above a solid base - echoed Utzon's Sydney Opera House concept of a cloud floating above a plateau or platform of functional purpose. It is one of the very few buildings in Sydney to extend Utzon's ideas in a meaningful way, into an entirely new urban context.[41]

In preparation for the Olympic year, Sydney gained from the strategic inclusion of major works of public

[39] Peter Spearritt, *Sydney's century: a history*. Sydney: UNSW Press, 1999; Geoffrey Moorhouse, *Sydney*, St Leonards, NSW: Allen & Unwin, 1999; Chris Johnson, *Shaping Sydney: public architecture and civic decorum*, Sydney: Hale & Iremonger, 1999; John Birmingham, *Leviathan: the unauthorised biography of Sydney*. Milsons Point, NSW: Random House, 1999; Lucy Turnbull, Lucy, *Sydney: biography of a city*, Milsons Point, NSW: Random House Australia, 1999; Patrick Bingham-Hall (ed.) and Chris Johnson, *Celebrating Sydney 2000: 100 legacies*, Sydney, NSW: Pesaro Publishing, 2000; John

Connell (ed.), *Sydney: the emergence of a world city*, Melbourne; Oxford: Oxford University Press, 2000.

[40] The complete political and design history of the urban plans for Homebush Bay, the successive and eventual Olympic bids based on that site, and the urban design processes that saw the completion of the site for 2000 is a complex story, yet to be written. For brief insight see, *Architecture Australia*, March/April 1996; and James Weirick, "Olympics Preview", Architecture Australia, May/June 1997, pp60-67. Chris Johnson's "Planning

the Olympic Site" in Patrick Bingham-Hall, *Olympic Architecture: Building Sydney 2000*, Sydney: Watermark Press, 1999, pp36-43, accurately presents the machinations surrounding the site which led directly to what was realised but it cannot, due to force of brevity, be regarded as presenting the most definitive historical account.

[41] The Olympic Park Railway Station gained state acclaim in 1998 as recipient of the RAIA's prestigious Sir John Sulman Medal and, in the same year, national acclaim as recipient of the Sir Zelman Cowen Award.

Foster St Apartment. Surry Hills, NSW. 1997.
Architect - Durbach Block

art and the physical revitalisation of some of its public institutions. While venerated monuments such as Hyde Park Barracks (1817-19), and the Customs House (1844, 1884), were refurbished as public exhibition spaces, others were developed privately.[42] The General Post Office (1864-91), for example, became a five star hotel, its postal hall transformed into a boutique-shopping mall and food court. On the water at Circular Quay, Lindsay and Kerry Clare acting for the NSW Government Architect, refurbished the ferry terminals. Nearby, the East Circular Quay development, controversial for its bulk and proximity to Utzon's Sydney Opera House, replaced a slim line of 1950s office slabs with a squat line of apartments and quickly earned for itself the nickname of the 'toaster'. The development was improved by Peddle Thorp's insertion of a lofty ground level colonnade, and its public redemption was aided by the writings on 19th century Colonial Architect James Barnet and civic decorum by academic Peter Kohane and the NSW Government Architect, Chris Johnson.[43] Their thesis was a vision of urban Sydney as a series of buildings with colonnades and shaded loggias that addressed the public spaces in front of these buildings, each façade becoming a magnificently modelled theatrical backdrop. At the same time, a spate of warehouse conversions in inner Sydney[44] signalled a shift in real estate concerns. Epitomising this shift was Durbach Block's Foster Street Apartment, Surry Hills (1997), a craggy outcrop clad in zinc and placed atop a tall brick warehouse, creating a new landscape silhouette.[45] Not only the coveted view of water now had value. There was at last a modest concession to urban conviviality, but it was still essentially private, discreet and responsible, and above all, exclusive.

Sydney was not alone in its city-centricity and water focus. In Brisbane, the redevelopment of South Bank under the direction of John Simpson, and the completion of Robin Gibson and Partners' design for the Queensland Cultural Centre in the late 1990s was another example of the city coming to the river. In Melbourne, the Crown Casino (1993-97), and Denton Corker Marshall's Melbourne Exhibition Centre (1996), were massive projects transforming the south bank of the Yarra River. This has continued with NMBW's black wedge insertion of the EQ restaurant/café (2001), under the balcony of Roy

[42] Hyde Park Barracks was restored and refurbished by Tonkin Zulaikha Harford and Clive Lucas in 1990-92. The Customs House was restored and refurbished by Tonkin Zulaikha and Jackson Teece Chesterman & Willis in 1998.
[43] Chris Johnson, Peter Kohane and Patrick Bingham-Hall, James Barnet : the universal values of civic existence, Sydney, NSW: Pesaro Publishing, 2000.
[44] Warehouse conversions designed by Kerridge Wallace Design Partnership, Jahn Associates, Sam Marshall, and Durbach Block were amongst the most outstanding examples in 1990s Sydney.
[45] Harry Margalit, Durbach Block: the luminous space of abstraction, Sydney, NSW: Pesaro Publishing, 1999.

Grounds' Melbourne Concert Hall (1981), at the eastern end of the stretch of river between Swanston Street and Spencer Street. At the western end, Peter Elliott has grafted a footbridge onto the Clarendon Street bridge, and a glazed screen wall and stairway (1998), onto the World Congress Centre. In each case, the river promenade and its flanking buildings have become a new public façade, an answer to the economically and politically driven strategies of urban renewal.[46] In other Australian cities, similar concepts have been investigated with varying degrees of success. Perth's design ideas competition for the broad stretch of parkland between the Swan River and the central business district faltered, while the popularity of the 19th century warehouse precinct of Salamanca Place on Hobart's waterfront as a place of recreation and retail continues unabated.

Further evidence of the dominant notion of 'centre' in terms of capital works has been the realm of corporate architecture. There is little international conception of what an Australian city looks like. Without exception, they are all sprawling conurbations with a central concentration of high rise buildings - skyscrapers that match any of the North American centres. In form, the late 20th century Australian city has no counterpart in Great Britain or Europe. Instead, cities like Vancouver, Houston, Toronto, Seattle, and Philadelphia come to mind, where the skyscraper is a clearly understood building form. Since the mid-1950s when height controls in Melbourne and Sydney were lifted from 40m (132 feet) and 46m (150 feet) respectively, in exchange for public open space at ground level, the shape of the Australian city has changed dramatically.[47] The Melbourne firm of Bates Smart and McCutcheon set the early pace with a series of high rise office slabs for the insurance group MLC across five capital cities. Its flagship, the MLC Building at North Sydney (1956), was a brilliant example of glazed curtain wall know-how. Their other works like ICI House, Melbourne (1959), briefly became beacons of a new corporate image for the Australian city, yet another mark of the postwar shift to a prevailing interest in things American. Successive collaborations during the 1960s with the Chicago and San Francisco offices of Skidmore Owings and Merrill

ICI Building. Melbourne, Vic. 1959.
Architect - Bates Smart McCutcheon

produced further diversity in skyscraper form and structure in Melbourne and Sydney.[48] Harry Seidler's Australia Square (1967), and MLC Centre (1978), became Sydney landmarks at sky level, and also at ground level with their generous landscaped plazas, while in the 1980s, Seidler designed sculpturally and structurally distinctive corporate office towers in Perth, Melbourne, Sydney, and Brisbane.[49]

By contrast, Perrott Lyon Mathieson's Telstra Corporate Centre in Exhibition Street, Melbourne (1992), and Denton Corker Marshall's Governor Phillip and Macquarie Towers, Sydney (1995), reflect a return to an

46 For example, Melbourne's South Bank is critically examined in terms of politics and urban space in Kim Dovey, Framing places: mediating power in built form, London; New York: Routledge, 1999.
47 Jennifer Taylor, Post World War II Multistoried Office Buildings in Australia 1945-1967 (Report prepared for The Australian Heritage Commission), Sydney: University of Sydney, April 1994.

48 Australian collaborations with Skidmore Owings and Merrill on high rise building designs include: Shell House, Melbourne, Victoria 1961 with Buchan Laird and Buchan; Wentworth Hotel, Sydney, NSW 1962-66 with Laurie and Heath; AMP Tower and St James, Melbourne, Victoria, 1965-69 with Bates Smart & McCutcheon; and BHP House, Melbourne, Victoria 1967-72 with Yuncken Freeman. In Melbourne, American

architect Harry Cobb (IM Pei) in association with Bates Smart & McCutcheon designed Collins Place 1970-80.
49 Grosvenor Place, Sydney, NSW 1982-88; Riverside Development, Brisbane, Queensland 1983-86; Capita Centre, Sydney, New South Wales 1984-89; Shell Headquarter, Melbourne, Victoria 1985-89; and QV1 Office Tower, Perth 1987-91.

Chifley Tower. 1993. Architect - Kohn Pedersen Fox/Travis Partners.
Aurora Place. 2001. Architect - Renzo Piano Building Workshop.
Governor Phillip Tower. 1995. Architect - Denton Corker Marshall.
Sydney, NSW.

idea of street architecture. These are soaring high rise office towers with skirts of low-rise offices at street level that restore the 19th century morphology of the generic city block. International architects have also contributed to the shape and profile of Australian city skylines, with towers by Kisho Kurokawa, Kohn Pederson Fox, and most recently, Renzo Piano, with his design for Aurora Place (2001), on Macquarie Street, Sydney. The Australian city of congestion is therefore like many other international centres of the New World. It is a high rise city of commercial speculation with increasingly, each tower harbouring - in the terms of Rem Koolhaas - its own "captive globe".[50] When complete, Nation Fender Katsalidis' World Tower in Sydney will be one of the tallest buildings in the Southern Hemisphere. Their Eureka Tower on the south bank of the Yarra River will form a new pole to Melbourne's skyline. Replacing the sole corporate tenant, there will now be a multitude of functions: residential, retail and commercial. These will be new worlds in the sky.

Southbank Arbour. Brisbane, Qld. 2000.
Architect - Denton Corker Marshall

From such a context comes the observation that, with the exception of one part of Melbourne's architecture culture, the dichotomy of centre and periphery is largely unaddressed in Australia. The outer suburban periphery still remains its own desert of architectural production, as does the vast acreage of the middle suburbs themselves where too few architectural works appear or even seem to be desired. All of this is concomitant with the global rise of the city-state generally in the 1990s.[51] In Australia this has meant the circumstantial rise of a generation of architects skilled in urban architecture and urban design, and in the growth of university courses in urban design. As planners have retreated into bureaucratic policy making and broad scale land and asset management, architects have been cast in additional roles as urban furniture makers, and as a corollary, designers of an extraordinary range of public domain architecture. Denton Corker Marshall's kilometre long serpentine pergola at South Bank in Brisbane, Tonkin Zulaikha's thirteen pylons marching down Olympic Boulevard at Homebush Bay, Buzacott Caro's footbridge to Darling Harbour in Sydney, and Wood Marsh's footbridge to the Docklands precinct in Melbourne signal a new competency and a new direction in sophistication and intensity, responding to the detail, scale and character of the Australian city.

King St Footbridge. Sydney, NSW. 1998.
Architect - Buzacott Caro

[50] In *Delirious New York: A Retroactive Manifesto for Manhattan* New York: Oxford University Press, 1978, p244, Rem Koolhaas proposes that "Each skyscraper – in the absence of real history – develops its own instantaneous 'folklore'. Through the double disconnection of *lobotomy and schism* – by separating exterior and interior architecture, and developing the latter in small autonomous instalments – such structures can devote their exteriors only to formalism and their interiors only to functionalism."
[51] See Saskia, Sassen, *The global city: New York, London, Tokyo*, Princeton, New Jersey: Princeton University Press, c1991; Saskia, Sassen, *Cities in a world economy*, Thousand Oaks, Calif.: Pine Forge Press, c1994; and Michael P Smith, *City, state, and market: the political economy of urban society*, New York, NY, USA: B. Blackwell, 1988.

LANDSCAPE AND SPACE

*Here pressed into the earth by the weight of that enormous
sky, there is real peace. To those who know it, the
annihilation of the self, subsumed into the vast emptiness
of nature, is akin to a religious experience. We children
grew up to know it and seek it as our father before us.*

Jil Ker Conway, The Road from Coorain(1989)[52]

If the periphery that is the suburbs remains untouched by architects, it may be because there is so much space beyond it. Australia is large and it has one of the lowest population densities in the world. There are vast tracts of sparsely populated agricultural pasturelands, and infinitely larger areas of untouched and unpopulated wilderness. While in Japan there is a cultural understanding of the space between things, in Australia there tends to be the reverse, a culture of objects, of the things themselves in space. Consequently the isolated object in an infinite landscape is not an uncommon occurrence. Nor is it an unusual conception from which to think about building in the Australia landscape.

The corrugated iron houses of Glenn Murcutt which 'touch the earth lightly'[53] are part of that tradition as are many (though not all) of the houses of Troppo, Gabriel Poole[54], Richard Leplastrier, and

[52] Jill Ker Conway, *The Road from Coorain*, London: Minerva, 1989 1993, p25

[53] See Philip Drew, "Touch this earth lightly", *The Architectural Review*, October 1988,

pp.90-91; and Philip Drew, *Touch this earth lightly : Glenn Murcutt in his own words*, Potts Points, NSW: Duffy & Snellgrove, 1999.

[54] Bruce Walker, *Gabriel Poole : space in which the soul can play*, Noosa, Queensland: Visionary Press, 1998.

Stutchbury and Pape[55]. For the most part, the landscape is left alone, untouched, evidence of a deliberately artless naturalism.[56] It is a relationship with the landscape that has its roots partly in the circumstantially straitened economies of post WWII 'difficult' sites in bush locations, gullies and precipitous slopes, and partly in the unselfconscious existentialism[57] of the architect-designed postwar house. This latter state was realised most fully in houses designed by architects for themselves, such as Bill and Ruth Lucas in Castlecrag, Sydney (1957), and John Hipwell in Warrandyte, Melbourne (1951). These were architects simply happy to be there in the trees,[58] or to be building in a modest clearing. The Australian bush was admitted as a backdrop to everyday living. There was no need to control it, instead a humble acknowledging of its greater force. There was also the added piquancy that the rationality and simplicity of the house's forms would be heightened against the contextless backdrop of Australia flora. Like the stripped Modernist forms of the buildings themselves, there was no historical association with such a landscape.

Yet this was not, and is not, the only position with respect to architecture mediating its presence within the Australian landscape. Ever since Arts and Crafts architects in Australia like Harold Desbrowe-Annear

Chadwick House. Eaglemont, Vic. 1903. Architect - Harold Desbrowe-Annear

and Alexander Stuart Jolly[59] began to build with materials and colours that were of the landscape itself, following a Ruskinian tradition of savage truthfulness, others have followed. An architecture that emerges almost directly from the landscape implies an organic and natural order. On the Castlecrag peninsula in Sydney, the 1920s houses of Walter Burley Griffin and Marion Mahony with their robust rock-faced walls and crystalline projections seemed to emerge directly from the earth.[60] The scoria-covered mushroom roof of Robin Boyd's Tower Hill Museum (1963-70), in Victoria's Western District echoed the undulation of the volcanic hills behind. Similarly, the undulating roofs of Gregory Burgess' Brambuk Living Cultural Centre at Halls Gap in the Grampians, Victoria (1990), seem not only to be remaking the

[55] Philip Drew, *Peter Stutchbury: of people and places : between the bush and the beach*, Sydney, NSW : Pesaro Publishing, 2000.
[56] Philip Goad, "New Land, New Language: Shifting Grounds in Australian Attitudes to Landscape, Architecture and Modernism 1940-1960", in Sean Pickersgill (ed.), *On What Ground(s)?*, Adelaide: Society of Architectural Historians, Australia and New Zealand, 1997, pp48-54.

[57] Ignasi de Sola-Morales Rubio, *Differences: topographies of contemporary architecture*, Cambridge, Mass.: MIT Press, 1997, pp41-55.
[58] I am grateful to Peter Brew and Toby Horrocks for independent but similar conversations and helpful observations on this concept of existentialism in postwar architecture culture.
[59] Jan Roberts (ed.), *Avalon : landscape and harmony : Walter Burley Griffin, Alexander Stewart Jolly & Harry Ruskin Rowe*, Avalon Beach, NSW: Ruskin Rowe Press, 1999.

[60] Meredith Walker, Meredith, Adrienne Kabos, and James Weirick, *Building for nature: Walter Burley Griffin and Castlecrag*, Castlecrag, NSW: Walter Burley Griffin Society, 1994; Anne Watson (ed.), *Beyond architecture: Marion Mahony and Walter Burley Griffin: America, Australia, India*, Haymarket, NSW: Powerhouse Publishing, 1998; Jeff Turnbull and Peter Y. Navaretti (eds.), *The Griffins in Australia and India : the complete works and projects of Walter Burley Griffin and Marion Mahony Griffin*, Melbourne: Miegunyah Press, 1998.

landscape, but they also recreate the camouflage mimicry of a giant moth. Such a tradition of direct physical engagement with the surrounding landscape continues. Kerstin Thompson's beach house at Lorne on Victoria's west coast can be read as a monumentalising of the cliff landscape and eroded rocks below. While at Lilydale, Victoria, Carey Lyon and Perrott Lyon Mathieson's Swinburne University building (1997), is a giant geological slice of landscape unearthed, revealing polychromatic subterranean striations on one side, and the contours of green roof on the other. Rather than stand delicately apart from the landscape, these buildings oscillate between topography and architecture, constantly raising the question of reciprocity between object and landscape.

Fishwick. Castlecrag, NSW.1929. Architect - Walter Burley Griffin and Marion Mahony

Another position with respect to the landscape, which is neither artless naturalism nor organic resonance, involves the creation of new landscapes, using both architecture and the manipulation of existing landscape to reshape a new one. In each case, the impetus may be different. Utzon's Sydney Opera House (1957-73), for example, floats above a massive man-made mesa that contains car parking and the seats of the auditoria.[61] Utzon created a new headland above an old one and then floated his own artificial sky over it. Denton Corker Marshall's house at Cowes, Phillip Island, Victoria (1991), and their Sheep House, Kyneton, Victoria (1998), involve incisions into the land, cuts and semi-burial.[62] It is the same notion that informs Mitchell Giurgola Thorp's semi-subterranean Parliament House, Canberra (1980-88), where a hill is removed and put back, eroded and then populated as a building.[63] Sean Godsell terraces the earth and partially embeds his battened and gridded houses that will eventually weather to blend with the land. Donovan Hill's workshop for the Architecture School at the University of Queensland campus, Brisbane, is the creation of an outdoor terrace above, and the continuation of a rock wall below. The workshop is simply the embedded space between. These are strategies tense with a knowledge that the indigenous people of Australia did not move the earth, but inhabited its clefts and caves, or built lightly and moved on. Remaking the landscape is not invalidated by such techniques. Its subtlety is measured by the final synthesis.

Tower Hill Natural History Centre. Koroit, Vic. 1963-70. Architect - Robin Boyd

There is a case for showing the markings of inhabitation. In the end, they may be more respectful than rising above the earth.

Other responses to landscape are the textured sound walls designed by Wood Marsh along Melbourne's Eastern Freeway and the rusted steel 'heaped earth' walls of their Shadowfax Winery at Werribee Park, Victoria. Kerstin Thompson's unbuilt project for RMIT's 'Long Life Loose Fit' building at the Bundoora campus

[61] Utzon's design method is best explained in his own words. See Jørn Utzon, "Platforms and Plateaus: Ideas of a Danish Architect", *Zodiac*, 10, 1962, pp112-140.   [62] Haig Beck and Jackie Cooper, *Denton, Corker, Marshall: rule playing and the rattbag element*, Boston, Mass.: Birkhauser, 2000.   [63] Haig Beck (ed.), *Parliament House, Canberra: A Building for the Nation*, Sydney: Watermark Press, 1988.

Glebe Island Arterial Sound Walls. Sydney, NSW. 1997. Architect/Artist - Richard Goodwin

in Melbourne's outer suburbs is a huge U-shape twisting along its length. These are pieces of virtual land art, giant markings on a landscape that is vast and sweeps through the suburban periphery. Each of these projects lies in a setting dense with other necessarily man-made markings of the landscape: the freeway, the cutting, the semi-rural fringe, and the earth berms of flyovers. There is a new perceptual awareness of landscape – that seen through the windscreen of the motor car. Similar ideas can be applied to inner urban locations. Inspired by the stylised atomic fission relief details of Walter Burley Griffin and Marion Mahony's Pyrmont incinerator (1935, demolished 1992), the concrete panels of Richard Goodwin's Glebe Island Arterial Sound Walls, Sydney (1997), become their own tattooed landscape. Here building has been transposed into useful trafficable contours.

In each of these positions with respect to the landscape, there should be acknowledged the notion of archipelago once again. The landscape of Australia is multi-faceted. No one landscape dominates, and no one spatial grain can be said to be consistent for its urbanised centres. Brisbane's hills and the disorienting serpentine meander of its river are one landscape. Sydney's harbour and the insistence on capturing the panorama is another, as is the relentless flatness of Melbourne's suburbs and the culture of the subdividing paling fence. The sand of Perth and the limited height of its brilliant indigenous flora are unlike anything on the east coast of Australia. In Darwin, the savannah landscape becomes instant jungle in the wet season. Each of the architectures in this book responds to the vagaries of a specific landscape. While the landscape myth of an Antipodean Arcadia is unified, in reality the conditions of landscape in Australia are multitudinous.

THE RISE OF THE UNIVERSITY

Across Australia, universities are building apace. Since the early 1990s, the competition for international students, research prestige, and a place in the increasingly lucrative tertiary education market has meant that more and more dollars are being spent on capital works for university campuses. High quality teaching and research spaces wrapped in a signature design have become a magic recipe. This boom in university buildings parallels a similar focus on the university in the 1950s and 1960s, when postwar tertiary education was a national priority, and there was a concerted campaign to not only revitalise existing campuses but to build entirely new universities.[64] It was a strategy based on building the so-called "clever country".

Startling pieces of progressive institutional architecture were produced.[65] These were buildings that sat outside the postwar demand for the single-family house, and the re-emergence of the corporate city building after World War II. University buildings set the pace in the postwar decades in terms of formal and structural experiment, the re-engagement with issues of civic monumentality and decorative ornament, urban design through campus planning, and the inclusion of progressive works of public art.[66] University buildings were then part publicly and part privately funded. Emphasis was given to quality and craftsmanship, material and formal longevity, and the need to complete or create precincts of building. The inclusion of considered landscape design was an intrinsic and guiding component to the work.

In the 1990s rise of the university, there have been similarities to the 1950s, though with altered emphasis. The shift of many technical colleges to university status[67] has meant that a corollary to the status change has been the desire to reform their visual image and their public presentation. No institution has been more active in that regard than the Royal Melbourne Institute of Technology, now RMIT University. A pivotal figure in that shift has been RMIT's Professor Leon Van Schaik, South African-born and London-trained, who deliberately shifted patronage away from establishment architecture firms who were following master plans that dated back to the late 1960s. He challenged the university hierarchy to commission progressive experimental designs from younger members of the profession.

Early yet discreet experiments included Ashton and Raggatt's refurbishment of RMIT Building 9 (1986), and Bates Smart and McCutcheon's wedge shaped lecture theatre (1991),[68] embedded within the firm's earlier megastructural 1965 and 1968 master plans.[69] The flagship, however, was RMIT Building 8 (1994), designed by Edmond and Corrigan in association with Demaine Partnership. The most extraordinary

---

[64] New postwar universities included: Australian National University, Canberra; Macquarie University and The University of New South Wales, Sydney; La Trobe and Monash Universities, Melbourne; Griffiths University, Queensland; and Edith Cowan and Murdoch Universities, Perth.

[65] For example, buildings such as James Birrell's Union College 1963-72 and JD Story Administration Building 1963 at the University of Queensland; the NSW Government Architect's Goldstein Hall at the University New South Wales 1963; Ken Woolley's design for the Fisher Library at the University of Sydney 1963 whilst working for the NSW Government Architect, and Ancher Mortlock Murray and Woolley's Student Union 1968

and Staff House 1969 at the University of Newcastle.

[66] Noteworthy pieces include Leonard French's mural "Triumph of Sport" in Eggleston McDonald and Secomb's Beaurepaire Centre, University of Melbourne, 1953-56 and Douglas Annand's figure emerging from ignorance towards enlightenment in Bates Smart and McCutcheon's Wilson Hall 1952-56 at the University of Melbourne. Note also the work of Tom Bass at the University of NSW; "The Falconer" 1955 and the sensuous reclining nude "Fountain Figure" 1959.

[67] From the 1970s onward, tertiary institutions such as Canberra College of Advanced Education, Gordon Institute of Technology, West Australian Institute of Technology, and

Queensland Institute of Technology began to change their status. Sydney Technical College had already changed, in 1949 when it was transformed into The University of New South Wales.

[68] Another early project for RMIT was Reed Mussen Styant Browne's RMIT Plumbing Building, Carlton, Victoria 1991.

[69] Nigel Bertram, "Institutional Imagings: Site and Desire in Swanston Street", in Leon van Schaik and Nigel Bertram (eds.), Building 8: Edmond and Corrigan at RMIT, vol.1, Melbourne: Schwarz Transition Monographs, 1996, pp26-37.

aspect of this project was its extremely public and colourful pronouncement of the University on Swanston Street, Melbourne's central civic and processional spine. Building 8 was compromised in practical ways by having to sit above an existing John Andrews-designed building (1977), accommodating its column grid and the minimum floor plates of adjacent Building 10. Yet Building 8's inclusivist referential language and bold public presence signalled new possibilities for university building in the early 1990s. When Ashton Raggatt McDougall's Storey Hall was completed next door in 1995, RMIT had in effect forged for itself a startling new and progressive image.[70] With the acquisition of suburban campuses at Bundoora and Brunswick, and the commissioning of buildings from a range of local and interstate architects[71], the Van Schaik strategy for RMIT University proved to be an outstanding public relations success. It had also ploughed the way for an entirely new culture in thinking about non-residential building in Victoria.

RMIT University was not alone in implementing such an identity change. Almost a decade before, Philip Cox had created the Haymarket Campus for the University of Technology, Sydney in 1980-84 in a mixed complex of historic buildings and new additions. The University of Newcastle had similarly commissioned a bright red building from high profile British architect Michael Wilford in 1989, and shortly afterward Grose Bradley and Stutchbury & Pape designed buildings for the same campus. In Perth, Cox Architects completed the New Technologies Building at Curtin University of Technology in 1993. What made the RMIT venture uniquely successful was not just the number of new buildings commissioned, but their persistent use of the professional media to broadcast this campaign and the frequency of professional awards gained by these buildings. Other universities have followed in varying degrees of haste, and the die was cast.[72]

Following a similar trajectory has been the upgrading of the TAFE (Technical and Advanced Further Education) colleges from technical schools where trade apprenticeships and vocational education were gained. Where these projects differ is firstly, the type of sites and landscape that these projects occupy - invariably on the periphery of the city, windswept and flat - and secondly, the budgets are less, but the spatial requirements greater as teaching spaces for trades and training require large robust shed-like spaces. At the same time, these institutions have the same desire as the university for the signature building. The buildings of Lyons Architects respond directly to this simultaneous challenge and limit. Their buildings celebrate their task of representation at the most graphic level and at the same time, acknowledge the expediency and constraints of contemporary building practice where standardised materials and conforming building practices dictate the banal detail. Buildings for tertiary education currently offer Australian architecture the greatest realm for experiment, and this is a directly desired client outcome.

[70] Other works on RMIT's city campus included the Faculty of Design, Cardigan Street by Allan Powell and Pels Innes Neilson and Kosloff 1996; Security Office, A'Beckett Street 1998, and Bowen Street urban design by Peter Elliott 1999.
[71] The list included Allan Powell, Peter Elliott, John Wardle, Lyons Architects, Durbach

Block, Wood Marsh with Pels Innes Neilson and Kosloff, and Kerstin Thompson.
[72] Peter Elliott's series of elegant new building grafts onto existing structures and Nonda Katsalidis's (later Nation Fender Katsalidis) Potter Gallery 1999 and Sidney Myer Asia Centre 2001 at the University of Melbourne have been part of this trend, as have been

recent buildings by Wood Marsh for Deakin University and RMIT, Jones Coulter Young in Western Australia for Edith Cowan University and Curtin University, in Brisbane, Donovan Hill for the University of Queensland, and Mitchell Giurgola Thorp for the University of New South Wales and The University of Sydney.

RMIT Building 8, Melbourne, Vic. 1994.
Architect - Edmond Corrigan with Demaine Partnership

THE HOUSE AS MODEL

73

In histories and commentaries on twentieth century Australian architecture, the detached single family house has almost always been invoked as the touchstone of experiment and innovation.[74] Robin Boyd's oft-quoted aphorism of 1952 that "Australia is the small house"[75] became the historian's crutch for much of the twentieth century. Early documentary works like Harold Desbrowe-Annear's journal 'For Every Man His Home' (1922)[76], and Sydney Ure Smith's 'Domestic Architecture in Australia' (1919)[77], reinforced this emphasis on the house. This is in complete contrast to writings on 19th century Australian architectural history that largely entailed the stylistic documentation of churches and public buildings. The picture of the 19th century was politely regarded as a succession of revival styles. Then, following the Pevsner model of writing history[78], the cleansing innocence of Arts and Crafts ideals was to release the house as the prophetic model of progressive development lurching towards the goal of International Modernism. Twentieth century discussions of the house have thus paralleled the documentation of Modernism in Australian architecture. As a result, the history of government and institutional Australian architecture of the twentieth century was, and has been, largely understudied. Robin Boyd's persuasive writings after 1947[79] and the desperate shortage of housing after World War II were largely to blame for the subsequent historiographic focus on the house for almost forty years.

Yet Boyd's aphorism was only part true. The distinctive feature of the continuing developments within contemporary Australian architecture is the exceptional quality of, and opportunity for,

73 Rose Seidler House. Wahroonga, NSW. 1950. Architect - Harry Seidler

74 For example, George, Beiers, *Houses of Australia: a survey of domestic architecture*, Sydney: Ure Smith, 1948; Kenneth McDonald, *The new Australian home*, Melbourne: K. McDonald, 1954; Neil Clerehan, *Best Australian houses : recent houses built by members of the Royal Australian Institute of Architects*, Melbourne: F.W.Cheshire, 1961; Jennifer Taylor, *An Australian identity: houses for Sydney, 1953-63*, Sydney: University of Sydney, Dept. of Architecture, 1972; Robert Irving, *Fine houses of Sydney*, Sydney: Methuen Australia, 1982; Robert Irving et al, *The History and Design of the Australian House*, Melbourne: Oxford University Press, 1985.

75 Robin Boyd, preface to *Australia's Home: Its Origins, Builders and Occupiers*, Carlton, Victoria: Melbourne University Press, 1952.

76 H. Desbrowe-Annear (ed.), *For every man his home: a book of Australian homes and the purpose of their design*, Melbourne: Alexander McCubbin, 1922.

77 Sydney Ure Smith (ed.) and Bertram Stevens in collaboration with W. Hardy Wilson, *Domestic Architecture in Australia*, Sydney: Angus and Robertson, 1919.

78 For writers like Robin Boyd after 1945, one of the most immediately available historical texts on modern architecture was Nikolaus Pevsner's *Pioneers of Modern Design from William Morris to Walter Gropius*, New York: Museum of Modern Art, 1949. This was the second edition, the first being published in 1936 under a slightly modified title. David Watkin analyses Pevsner's mode of art historical writing in "Architectural Writing in the 1930s", *Architectural Design*, October 1979; *Morality and architecture: the development of a theme in architectural history and theory from the Gothic revival to the modern movement*, Oxford: Clarendon Press, 1977; and *The Rise of Architectural History*, London: The Architectural Press, 1980.

79 Robin Boyd's publishing output between 1947 and 1971, mainly as a critic and commentator rather than as an historian, was extraordinary. In that time, he wrote twelve books and for almost ten consecutive years, he wrote a weekly newspaper article on architecture.

freestanding architect-designed houses, often sited in virgin landscapes. There is no doubt that Australian architecture is separated from much of the rest of the world's architecture, including the United States, by the continuing affordability of land and the opportunity to build upon it afresh. So while theoretical revisionists might deplore the continuing domestic focus of awards programs and magazine reviews, the detached house continues to be an intrinsic part of the architecture (and popular) culture in Australia. The model of the house remains as one of the fundamental experimental grounds for any Australian practice of any size.

Oribin Studio. Cairns, Qld. 1963.
Architect - Eddie Oribin

When an architect builds his own home, it may be assumed that the false influences of economic expediency depart and leave him as free to create as a painter at his blank canvas, as a musician or a poet.... In his own home all his philosophy of building must surely blossom, if ever it us to. Here he is both playwright and actor, composer and executant. What manner of architect he is will be laid bare for all the world to see...

Robin Boyd, Victorian Modern (1947)[80]

Buhrich House. Castlecrag, NSW. 1972.
Architect - Hugh Buhrich

Anselm. Caulfield, Vic. 1906.
Architect - Robert Haddon

McIntyre House. Kew, Vic. 1955.
Architect - Peter and Dione McIntyre

Central to the notion of the house as laboratory of ideas is the phenomenon of the architect's own house. These are works that are extremely personal and at the same time potential show pieces, exemplary publicity for the architect's practice. Many of these architects' own homes have become pivotal moments in the history of Australian architecture. From Robert Haddon's Free Style 'Anselm', in suburban Caulfield, Melbourne (1906), Leslie Wilkinson's romantic Mediterranean Revival version of the Colonial Georgian, 'Greenway' in Sydney's Vaucluse (1923), Hardy Wilson's prim American version of the Colonial Georgian, 'Purulia', Wahroonga, Sydney, (1916), Peter and Dione McIntyre's daring structural-functional house pinned like a butterfly to the slope in Kew (1955), Peter Muller's oversailing and intersecting roof planes amidst the angophoras at Whale Beach, Sydney (1955), Neville Gruzman's compacted Usonian masterpiece in Darling Point, Sydney (1958), Eddie Oribin's house and studio in Cairns (1963), to Hugh Buhrich's live-in sculpture at Castlecrag, Sydney (1972), the list is endless.[81] At the same time, unbuilt houses designed by architects for themselves are equally potent, witness Jørn Utzon's unbuilt project

[80] Robin Boyd, *Victorian Modern*, Melbourne: Victorian Architecture Students Society, 1947, p51.

[81] Other architects who have designed important houses for themselves include: Rex Addison, Harold Desbrowe-Annear; Robin Boyd, Peter Brew, Peter Carmichael, Kai Chen, Lindsay and Kerry Clare, Neil Clerehan, Marshall Clifton; Philip Cox, Don Gazzard, Walter Burley Griffin and Marion Mahony, Roy Grounds, John James, Raymond Jones, Bill and Ruth Lucas, Jack McConnell, Michael Markham, Barrie Marshall, Glenn Murcutt, Gabriel Poole, Desmond Sands; Harry Seidler, and Ken Woolley.

for his family at Bayview, Sydney (1961-65), a thorough-going essay in earth-bound return brick walls with a floating roof of bent plywood sections.[82]

In the late 1990s, such a tradition is maintained. In each of these recent houses, what is at stake is not just the architect's own reputation but also a whole raft of ideas. For the most part, these houses are a celebration of the individual and idiosyncratic (in the positive sense) personal experiments that explore ideas and take risks. It might just be that the exception becomes the rule, the model. Brit Andresen and Peter O'Gorman's house of repetitive vertical timber members at Mooloomba on Stradbroke Island, Queensland, for example, represents the architects' long-held interest in harmonic proportions, the intrinsic merits of Australian hardwoods, and the timeless value of placemaking. John Wardle's house in Kew is the reworking of and addition to an existing 1950s house designed by Horace Tribe. It is another experiment in timber construction, but also a masterly display of Wardle's intense affair with detail and the sequential experience of the threshold. The reverberations of intent can then be seen in works subsequent to these houses. The same can be said of each of the architect's own houses in this book. Each becomes a catalyst in the architect's oeuvre for change, release, and creative escape.

At the same time as architects explore the limits of their ability to be accommodated within their own creations, there are clearly other interests in the design of houses. The idealistic Modernist theme of a house for everyman during the 1950s had as its logical outcome, the project houses of the 1960s and 1970s. There has been a different focus to the 1990s. With few exceptions, the notion of social idealism has been approached in another way. As the speculative builder has been regarded for the most part as invincible, architects designing one-off houses have been largely restricted to four areas of production.

Firstly, for the middle and upper class market, able to afford single family houses, there has been the traditional notion of the suburban villa. Stutchbury and Pape's Bay House, Donovan Hill's celebrated

Bay House. Watsons Bay, NSW. 2001. Architect - Stutchbury & Pape

⁸² Kenneth Frampton, *Studies in Tectonic Culture: The Poetics of Construction in Nineteenth and Twentieth Century Architecture*, Cambridge, Mass.: MIT Press, 1995, pp268-269, 271; Philip Drew, *The Masterpiece: Jørn Utzon: a secret life*, South Yarra, Victoria: Hardie Grant Books, 1999, pp374-378.

C House, and Wood Marsh's Gottleib House are the grand examples. Even these impeccably conceived and detailed houses are limited by subdivision lot sizes, and the realities of a house-commissioning public less able to afford generous sites close to the central city. These houses and others like them are becoming increasingly rare in Australia. Like vintage sports cars, their aspirations for performance, look, and longevity are pure. The sheer sculptural formalism of the Gottleib House, the controlling and defining monumentalising of the 'outdoor' internal volume of the C House, and the exquisitely crafted structure and operable glass/shade walls of the Bay House are explored to maximum effect.

By contrast, in a second avenue of practice, many architects are finding commissions for beach houses. In Australia, the idea of the beach house, both modest and grand, dates back to the 19th century, and as a tradition, the cult of the beach house has enjoyed sustained popularity. To escape from Brisbane to the Sunshine Coast, from Melbourne to the Mornington Peninsula or the Great Ocean Road, to escape Perth and head south towards Margaret River, or to head north or south from Sydney, and arrive at a beach house is part of what summer holidays are about, and for many people, this is what living in Australia means. This idea is so strong in some cases, that the elements held so dear to the beach house – experimental open planning, outdoor rooms and capacious decks, informal spatial and functional delineations, and a relaxed palette of furnishings and materials - have made their way into everyday domestic design.[83] This is especially so in houses designed by Stutchbury and Pape for idyllic sites on the northern beaches of Sydney. In many of these houses, the analogy of the perpetual beach house is not loosely made. The towel hanging on the balustrade, the sand on the timber deck, and the glass sliding door evoke very specific images of living near water and sun.

While the 1950s seemed to epitomise the egalitarian era of a beach shack that was affordable to many, the situation today has changed. The newly commissioned beach house is, by and large, a rare privilege. For those clients who can afford it, the notion of apartment or town house living in the city can have a necessary outlet in the bush retreat, but more commonly in the beach house. They are not so much holiday houses as second houses, substantial alternatives to the city, houses that encompass different evocations of dwelling. They are less formal, less materially precious, have looser notions of propriety, and above all, make a serious engagement with the coastal landscape and the prospect of a vista.

The architect's third avenue of house production is the warehouse/factory conversion. With the rapid rise in popularity of inner city living since the 1980s, the conversion of former industrial and commercial buildings to residences has become a market in itself. As the building stock is neither consistent nor formally predictable, an architect's skill is highly desirable. Additionally, as arguments for sustainable

⁸³ Robin Boyd was to suggest a similar idea in 1950 in "Mornington Peninsula", *Architecture*, 38, 4, October-December 1950, pp148-152.

Drum House. Fitzroy, Vic. 2001. Architect - Kerstin Thompson

development begin to dominate discussions of planning and urban design in the older and denser cities of Sydney, Melbourne, Brisbane and Fremantle, the conversion of existing building stock has developed its own traditions. In Melbourne especially, where demand on former industrial and commercial space is less than that of Sydney, architects have proved that the opportunity to sacrifice outdoor open space for a large internal volume has not meant a reduction in the architectural value of the work. Rather, there is the potential for a new series of spatial and formal relationships to be formed, especially in terms of what a dwelling space might mean, and how existing non-residential fabrics might be drawn into becoming signifiers of home. Kerstin Thompson's Drum House, for example, is the reconfiguration of a sheet metal factory. What is ingenious and imaginative about this conversion is that the warehouse has not been dramatically reshaped to become a house - there is no attempt to make the space masquerade as a typical house. Ignoring the typical response of inserting a smart interior design within an existing shell, Thompson has built a glazed drum as an internal court and daylight lantern within the warehouse volume. It is a large-scale statement where home is achieved by the occupation of residual spaces surrounding the insertion of the glazed drum.

The fourth avenue in terms of the architect-designed house is the literal idea of the house as a model for larger or repetitive work, or the development of a type. Some of these houses such as Donovan Hill's D House, have implications for medium density housing or small lot houses. Sean Godsell's houses explore the notion of corridor-less houses. Others like Engelen Moore's Price/O'Reilly House offer themselves as set pieces, iconic units that beg repetition, stacking, or an exploding of scale to become larger multiple dwelling types. This is not a new idea in terms of the house.[84] They are propositional types, polemical one-off houses that are dense with immanence. They are not intended to be personal statements. Like Sean Godsell's Future Shack, a shipping container that houses a temporary shelter for disaster-struck people around the world, such houses point to the continuing validity of the house as a key element to the relevance of architectural artifice.

84 Le Corbusier's Pavilion Esprit Nouveau in Paris (1925), many of the 1950s Los Angeles *Arts and Architecture* Cast Study Houses, and more recently, in Melbourne, Hamish Lyon and Astrid Jenkin's own house in Carlton, (1993, in association with Charles Salter) and FIELD's Holyoake House, Hawthorn, (2000) challenge the status quo and suggest themselves as models for new ways of thinking about the house/dwelling.

MODELS OF HOUSING

The 20th century historiographic focus on the single-family house has meant the neglect of the study of multiple housing in Australia, despite a range of extraordinary examples,[85] and the rapid urban consolidation of its coastal cities. World War II effectively broke the evolutionary development of multiple dwelling types that had occurred from the 1910s to the late 1930s. In those decades virtually every state capital city experienced the invention and experiment with, and adoption of, new and denser living patterns. Additionally, the Anglo-Saxon stigma of collective dwelling was gradually eroded as these new building types found favour with the fashionable, wealthy, young and upwardly mobile members of society. The locations of the apartments were predicated on proximity to train and tram routes, strip-shopping streets and public parks.

Wyldefel Gardens. Potts Point, NSW. 1936.
Architect - WA Crowle with John Brogan

Newington Apartments (Olympic Village). Newington, NSW. 1999-2000. Architect - Bruce Eeles with HPA

The flashy Hollywood-inspired Beverley Hills apartment block in South Yarra, Melbourne (1936), with 'ye olde swimming pool' and the Moderne style Birtley Towers in Potts Point, Sydney (1936), suggested new ways of living. Experiments in housing typology were thus not limited in style to the serious Functionalist experiments that included Taylor Soilleux and Overend's *existenzminimum* Cairo flats in Fitzroy, Melbourne (1935-36), with their flat roofs, porthole windows, and cantilevered concrete access walkways and private balconies. Similar Functionalist examples could be found in Perth by Krantz and Sheldon, in Adelaide by Jack McConnell, and in Potts Point, Sydney, with the wonderful Wyldefel Gardens (1936), designed by JR Brogan and his client W.A.L. Crowle. This latter development was closely examined by Bruce Eeles and HPA Architects in the design and construction of the walk-up apartments at Homebush Bay (1999-2000), for the Sydney Olympic Games.

It is not only these models from the 1930s that now attract interest and admiration from architects. Isolated examples from the 1940s, 1950s and 1960s, previously unassimilated into orthodox architectural histories now beg documentation. JW Rivett's Caringal flats, Toorak, Melbourne (1948-51); Aaron Bolot's

[85] Exceptions to this lack of study of multiple dwellings in Australia include: Terry Sawyer; Residential flats in Melbourne: the development of a building type to 1950, BArch Research Report, University of Melbourne, 1982 and Donald Dunbar; Australian flats: a comparison of Melbourne and Sydney flat developments in the interwar period, PhD Thesis, University of Melbourne, 1998.

Wylde Street Apartments. Potts Point,
NSW. 1951. Architect - Aaron Bolot

Wylde Street apartments, Potts Point, Sydney (1951); Neville Gruzman's startlingly minimal Montrose apartments, Neutral Bay (1955); Job and Froud's massive Torbreck in Highgate Hill, Brisbane (1961); Bernard Joyce and Bill Nankivell's rigorous exploration of the speculative apartment in 1960's Melbourne, and especially Harry Seidler's relentless development of the apartment type from the 1950s to the 1990s, are potential candidates for further study. All point to a history of medium and high density housing that paralleled the much publicised disasters of subsidised multiple dwelling projects by state government housing commissions,[86] and the much-maligned speculative 'six pack' flats that proliferated from the 1950s to the 1970s in every Australian capital city.

In the 1990s, medium and high-density housing has come into stark focus in the Australian city. Moves towards urban consolidation promoted at federal and local government level have meant that the functionally zoned city of the 1960s is being progressively reoccupied. In short, the city is being redefined. Not all the high rise housing blocks qualify as reputable architecture, and many of the developments have been controversial for their placement within sensitive inner urban neighbourhoods, a practice that since the 1970s has at times drawn drastic union action and community resistance.[87] However, in the last decade Australian architecture has experienced a minor revolution in apartment building design, and with the conversion of former industrial building stock and obsolete 1950s and 1960s office towers into housing.

Montrose Apartments. Neutral Bay, NSW. 1955.
Architect - Neville Gruzman

In Melbourne, the series of more than a dozen exuberant apartment buildings by Nonda Katsalidis (later Nation Fender Katsalidis) must be considered a remarkable phenomenon. 170 La Trobe Street (1991); Melbourne Terraces (1994); Richmond Silos (1996), St Leonards Apartments, St Kilda (1996), Spring Street Apartments (1999), and the Republic Tower (2000), have all been designed on the basis of a richly modelled external surface, often accompanied by the inclusion of discrete pieces of public art and artist-executed decorative finishes. These buildings include robust interior shells able to take a further Katsalidis layer, or in a savvy real estate gesture, new owners can fit out the shell for themselves. The success of the Katsalidis model is indisputable. Residents are able to live in a signature building, a landmark, thereby avoiding the stigma of faceless anonymity so long attached to 1960s high-rise housing blocks, yet still be able to express their own interior design preference. Nation Fender Katsalidis have made apartment living fashionable, and simultaneously, a lucrative investment

[86] For two cases of state-subsidised housing programs, see Renata Howe (ed.), *New houses for old : fifty years of public housing in Victoria, 1938-1988*, Melbourne: Ministry of Housing and Construction, 1988; Susan Marsden, *Business, charity and sentiment: the South Australian Housing Trust, 1936-1986*, Netley, South Australia: Wakefield Press, 1986.

[87] For example in Sydney, the Victoria Street project, Kings Cross in the 1970s was an extremely controversial development proposed by developer Frank Theeman. One of the project's most vocal opponents was newspaper journalist Juanita Nelson who mysteriously disappeared during the affair and whose body was never found. Union activity was also strong in its opposition in Sydney to building proposals for The Rocks in the 1970s. See Marion Hardman and Peter Manning, *Green Bans: The Story of an Australian Phenomenon*, East Melbourne, Victoria, Australian Conservation Foundation, 1975.

Republic Tower, Melbourne, Vic. 2000.
Architect - Nonda Katsalidis

alternative. Their two towers, the Eureka in Melbourne and World Tower in Sydney, will be two of the tallest residential tower blocks in Australia, and in effect the ultimate expression of the shift in Australian notions of what home might mean.

A variation on this theme, based partly on fashion as well as notions of repetition and the disciplined refinement of type, can be observed in the work of Engelen Moore in Sydney. Their highly visible and well publicised designs for the Altair, Grid, and Barcom Avenue apartments are the outcome of experiments in one-off housing and the firm's strong interest in, and commitment to, prefabricated joinery and bathroom units. Standardisation and material economies are combined with shrewd yet disarmingly simple urban strategies. The placement of the Altair apartments above a road tunnel, and the graphic placement of the giant brise-soleil, or sunscreen, across its front reads like a billboard from the highway. Similar in appearance, but not layout, is the Republic development in Darlinghurst, Sydney (2001), by Burley Katon Halliday. There, the glistening white (some might say over-glazed) harbourside apartment has been transported and multiplied onto a gritty inner urban site. These Melbourne and Sydney

Altair Apartments. Kings Cross, NSW. 2001. Architect - Engelen Moore

practices highlight extreme differences in the aesthetics of multiple housing - the key is diversity and spatial invention within tight market and demographic constraints. While these apartments are almost all speculative, rather than affordable housing (the dominant focus from the 1950s to the early 1970s), they signal a return to the civilised urbs that was the Australian metropolis as it had developed up to the late 1920s. Today, however, the language of architectural 'civility' is completely new.

DEFINING
ABORIGINAL ARCHITECTURE

The awareness of and response to an architecture for and of indigenous Australia has been a long time coming, and is a long time overdue. With the exception of socio-anthropological texts, no general history of Australian architecture entertained or included within its ambit the notion of an indigenous architectural tradition until John Archer's 'Building a Nation' in 1987.[88] Robin Boyd in 1952 had been positively dismissive of any notion of such a tradition.[89] The architectures of the missions and government housing in outback and northern Australia from the 1920s to the 1950s were unremarkable structures and spaces laden with years of occasionally misinformed charity, and at times, ill-conceived social engineering. In the 1960s, there were isolated moments of true engagement at an architectural and social level such as Joyce Nankivell's Aboriginal Community Centre, Northcote, Melbourne (1963), with its warped plywood roof. But it was not until the early 1970s that, as Paul Memmott has observed, "after a series of classical failures (houses destroyed and abandoned), it was realised that culturally appropriate design would have to be based on a detailed understanding of aboriginal shelter and settlement relations".[90]

Ngaripuluwamigi Nguiu. Bathurst Island (1973-82).
Architect - Peter Myers

Ngaripuluwamigi Nguiu.

The 1980s saw concerted research into indigenous architecture at a practical and academic level. One of the earliest practical collaborations with indigenous people was Peter Myers' Ngaripuluwamigi Nguiu (Keeping Place) on Bathurst Island (1973-82), for the Tiwi Aboriginal community.[91] Peter Myers was sent to Bathurst Island in 1973 by the Aboriginal Arts Board of the Australia Council to hold initial dialogues with the Tiwi people. The resulting building was a simple open prefabricated steel structure with a plywood barrel-vaulted interior volume. A softly curving corrugated steel roof is wrapped over it, a modern echo of the sheet bark structures of the Tiwi people erected annually for Kulama, the ceremony held to celebrate the ripening and harvesting of the indigenous yams. Other projects like

[88] John Archer, *Building a Nation: a history of the Australian house*, Sydney : Collins, 1987
[89] Robin Boyd, in *Australia's Home*, Melbourne University Press, 1952, p123, describes the Australian aborigines as having no use for "the house, the home, the permanent address – this was the white man's idea". Yet, Boyd does acknowledge the occupation of "a hollow tree or a cave, or behind a low breakwind of boughs set with prophetic accuracy against the force of the coming night wind." Boyd also comments on their skilful use of bark for canoes and "open-fronted tribal huts".

[90] Paul Memmott, "Contemporary Aboriginal Architecture", *The Architectural Review*, 1100, September 1988, p87.
[91] Peter Myers, in Robert Edwards and Jenny Stewart (eds), *Preserving Indigenous Cultures: A New Role for Museums*, Canberra: UNESCO-AGPS, 1980.

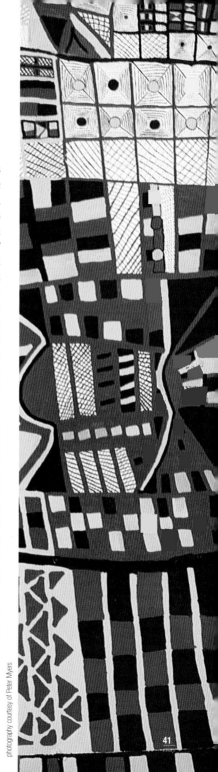

photography courtesy of Peter Myers

Aboriginal Alcoholic Rehabilitation Centre (unbuilt). Kinchela, NSW. 1988.
Architect - Glenn Murcutt. photography © Max Dupain & Associates

Gregory Burgess' Brambuk Living Cultural Centre, Halls Gap, Gariwerd (Grampians National Park) in Victoria (1990), and Glenn Murcutt's unbuilt Aboriginal Alcoholic Rehabilitation Centre, Kinchela, NSW (1988), demonstrate the two major formal differences in approaching design for indigenous communities. Both involved close community consultation and collaboration in the design process, but have radically different formal outcomes. In Burgess' case, the results are invariably figurative and anthropomorphic in allusion. In their later works and collaborations with indigenous clients, these differences become accentuated. At Uluru (Ayers Rock) in the Northern Territory, the Uluru-Kata Tjuta Aboriginal Cultural Centre (1995), is literally an image of two snakes not touching, but inextricably in dialogue. By contrast, Murcutt's much celebrated Marmburra Marika and Mark Alderton House, Yirrkala, Northern Territory (1993), arose not just through allusion to traditional Aboriginal forms of shelter, but from Murcutt's intensely personal investigation of the linear house as a constant model for dwelling. These Burgess and Murcutt projects, in many respects the most strongly formalistic and aesthetically resolved responses to indigenous architecture, are also those avidly devoured by the professional press in search of visual 'answers' to the wants of Australia's indigenous people. Occasionally, critics have pondered this dilemma, but in doing so have inadvertently cast such high profile architects in a negative light, when in fact it is an image-hungry media that produces the tension.[92] Often overlooked is the validity and ongoing testing of multiple models for approaching the notion of an architecture for and of Australia's indigenous people.

The directions followed in the last ten years have also built upon important research by Paul Memmott at the University of Queensland. For more than twenty years he has detailed the form and growth of aboriginal settlements.[93] His pioneering contributions have ensured a comprehensive basis to understanding cultural issues in relation to questions of indigenous settlement and attitudes to space. Also critical has been research carried out by Paul Pholeros in the early 1980s, not positing "the house itself as a finite object, rather… the process of providing and using houses"[94] within the Anangu Pitjantjatjara lands. Pholeros' kit of parts model and his attempts to address fundamental issues of health were explored in his Mutitjulu Community Housing project at Uluru, Northern Territory (1987). This research was elaborated further in his 1993 book 'Housing for Health'[95] which has become a standard reference for understanding some of the most basic issues involved in practising with and within an Aboriginal community. Also influential has been the output of the Aboriginal-controlled design practice of Tangentyere Aboriginal Council, based in Alice Springs, where commitment to a high degree of direct consultation, participation, and specific culturally appropriate responses wrought a consistent degree of client approval and sensitive architecture.[96] With the support of the Council's Aboriginal executive and

[92] K Dovey, "Architecture and Aborigines", *Architecture Australia*, 85, 4, 1996; M Lochert, "Mediating Aboriginal Architecture", *Transition*, 54/55, 1997; K Dovey, J Jacobs, and M Lochert, "Authorising Aboriginality in Architecture", in L Lokko (ed), *White Papers, Black Marks: Architecture, Race, Culture*, London, The Athlone Press, 2000, pp218-235.
[93] Paul Memmott's writings include: "Aboriginal Housing: The State of the Art (or the Non-state of the Art), *Architecture Australia*, June 1988, pp34-47; "The development of Aboriginal Housing Standards in Central Australia: The Case Study of Tangentyere

Council", in B Judd and P Bycroft (eds.), *Evaluating Housing Standards and Performance* (Housing Issues 4), RAIA National Education Division, Canberra, 1989, pp115-143; *Humpy, house and tin shed : Aboriginal settlement history on the Darling River*, Sydney : Ian Buchan Fell Research Centre, Faculty of Architecture, University of Sydney, 1991; "Remote prototypes", *Architecture Australia*, May/June 2001, pp60-65.
[94] Rory Spence, "Health hardware", *The Architectural Review*, October 1988, pp92-93.

The *Environmental and Public Health Review within the Anangu Pitjantjatjara Lands* was conducted in 1986-87.
[95] Paul Pholeros, Stephan Rainow, Paul Torzillo, *Housing for health: towards a healthy living environment for Aboriginal Australia*, Newport Beach, NSW : Healthabitat, c1993
[96] Jane Dillon and Mark Savage, "Tangentyere Council", *The Architectural Review*, October 1988, pp926-97.

under the stewardship of Jane Dillon and Mark Savage, and later Deborah Fisher and Sue Dugdale, Tangentyere Design has come to be seen as a landmark practice.

Recent works in the Northern Territory and Queensland by Troppo, Deborah Fisher, Danny Wong, and Simon Scally for remote communities in Arnhem Land, and on islands in the Gulf of Carpentaria, have been part of a conscientious attempt to find various paths towards reconciling the failures and missed opportunities of past design methods. Other important projects include those in Victoria, by Gregory Burgess, Peter Sanders and Anthony Styant-Browne[97]; and in New South Wales, the additions to Tranby Aboriginal Co-operative in Glebe, inner Sydney (1998), by Cracknell Lonergan with the Merrima Unit of the NSW Department of Public Works, and the latter unit's design for the Girrawaa Creative Work Centre outside Bathurst Gaol, Bathurst, New South Wales (1998)[98]. Some of the projects have been housing, some have been concerned with the representation of Aboriginality, while others have addressed the representation of a particular place. One project that gained national attention was Troppo and Glenn Murcutt's Bowali Visitor Information Centre at Kakadu National Park, Northern Territory (1994). It is notable not just for its formal dexterity, but also for its programmatic success as being truly representative of an extraordinary natural landscape inhabited by indigenous people.

Contemporary projects for indigenous people over the last five years have been important for bringing such architecture to broad public attention. However it must be stressed that so much of this architectural work is not seen. It is too remote. It is not necessarily formally dramatic, but quiet and pragmatic. So much of the dilemma of Aboriginal housing and settlement is invisible. The feting of one or two signal projects has been the surrogate for a practice intensely collaborative, humbling, and labour intensive. Perhaps the most potent symbol of all of these initiatives has been the Aboriginal Tent Embassy in Canberra, which was erected in 1977 in the grounds directly opposite John Smith Murdoch's prim provisional Parliament House (1927).[99] The Tent Embassy's continued presence is testament to the fact that any new directions in Australian cultural life, and by extension into the realm of architecture cannot ignore a constant dilemma: that European settlement and its traditions of building come into direct conflict with a people whose land is no longer their own.

[97] The Galeena Beek Living Cultural Centre, Healesville 1996 was designed by Anthony Styant-Browne. See K Dovey, 'Aboriginal Cultural Centres', in S Kleinert and M Neale (eds), *The Oxford Companion to Aboriginal Art and Culture*, Melbourne: Oxford University Press, 2000, pp419-423.
[98] The Merrima Unit of the NSW Department of Public Works and Services was created in 1995. The unit is directed by three Aboriginal architect/designers: Dillon Kombumerri, Kevin O'Brien, and Alison Page. For information on works by the unit, see Chris Johnson, *Shaping Sydney: public architecture and civic decorum*, Sydney: Hale & Iremonger, 1999, pp213-216. See also *Architecture Australia*, 87:3 (May/June 1998); and 87:5 September/October 1998.
[99] Tent embassies also appeared in Adelaide, 13 July 1972, Perth, outside the Western Australian Parliament June 1972, and two locations in Sydney, New South Wales – Mrs Macquarie's Chair 26 January 1988 and Victoria Park, near Broadway 14 July 2000.

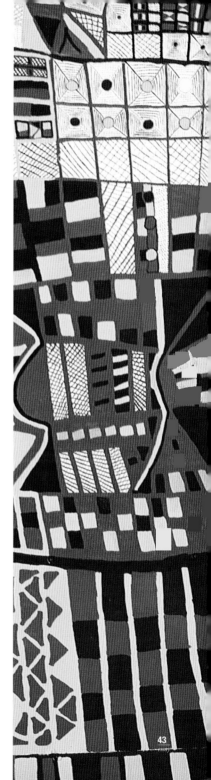

THE PERSISTENCE OF DESIGN TRADITIONS

100

In September 1951, Robin Boyd wrote of "A New Eclecticism?"[101] in the English periodical, The Architectural Review. As an Australian writing in the hallowed pages of that journal, Boyd verged on the dangerously gauche with his invocation of the term 'eclecticism'. Few would dare do it today. Yet his thesis was accurate - that the trajectory of Modernism had reached a point of unlimited choice - so why shouldn't an architect be free to choose the mood or metre in which to operate? Further proof of Boyd's argument has been the fact that the technology of building construction has not developed dramatically in the last fifty years. Architecture, or the act of building, has become one of society's most anachronistic activities, a process still largely done by hand, with its materials largely drawn from the same palette as fifty years before. Thus while the theories underpinning architecture have skittered across new dimensions, traditions of design composition have tended to stay the same.

Accepting this proposition, the new directions in Australian architecture of the last ten years have seen the parallel consolidation of various ways of designing an object. While the processes of design have become infinitely more sophisticated, the formalism of the outcome has tended to remain within conventional understandings of what a building might be. This is not a disturbing prognosis, but it is symptomatic of architectural production the world over. Commonly acknowledged is the diminution of the position of social conscience in architecture. An endearing conceit of Modernism was its perceived social role. With the rise in doubt, and the evident humility in the face of the over-ambitious

[100] D House, New Farm, Qld. 2000. Architect - Donovan Hill
[101] Robin Boyd, "A New Eclecticism?", *The Architectural Review*, 110, 657, September 1951, pp150-153.

social program of architectural Modernism, there comes in its place, a suspicion of idealistic posturing and the relevance of architecture as a panacea to various social ills. The political economies of construction have shifted dramatically. Craft has dimmed, and expediency has risen in stature. This is a reality. Despite this, now evident in Australian architecture is the persistence and resilience of three major compositional traditions. It must be said that these traditions are of equal value - eagerly followed, hotly contested, zealously rejected – and this makes Australian architecture distinctive. Arguably, the only other country to pursue a similar experience is Japan, though for entirely different material and cultural reasons. Each of these three traditions arises from essentially post-1945 concerns - another distinctly Australian characteristic - where the basis of the culture is consistently updating itself within the confines of "anxious modernisms"[102], already self-critical rather than utopic in vision.

THE TECTONIC

The first tradition concerns the strength and survival of the tectonic in architecture. The word 'tectonic' has a number of meanings.[103] In this case, Kenneth Frampton's definition, derived from Eduard Sekler, is the most useful. Tectonic can be defined as "a certain expressivity arising from the statical resistance of constructional form in such a way that the resultant expression could not be accounted for in terms of structure and construction alone."[104] This approach to structure and materials is the self-sustaining and conforming image of what Australian architecture apparently should be, and its virtues are internationally well known and understood. With its roots in the clear structural and material integrity of houses like Bill and Ruth Lucas' house at Castlecrag, Sydney (1957), the institutional buildings of Frederick Romberg, and the houses of Gabriel Poole, Rex Addison, Russell Hall, Glenn Murcutt, and Richard Leplastrier, the belief in an ontology or essential nature of construction is pervasive.[105]

Addison House. Taringa, Qld. 1999. Architect - Rex Addison

[102] For an account of the 'anxiety' of postwar Modernism, see Sarah Williams Goldhagen and Réjean Legault, "Introduction: Critical Themes of Postwar Modernism", *Anxious Modernisms: Experimentation in Postwar Architectural Culture*, Montreal: Canadian Centre for Architecture; Cambridge: MIT Press, 2000, pp13-21.
[103] For an overview of the various meanings attached to the term 'tectonic', see Kenneth Frampton, "Introduction: Reflections on the Scope of the Tectonic", *Studies in tectonic*

culture: the poetics of construction in nineteenth and twentieth century architecture, Cambridge, Mass.: MIT Press, 1995, pp1-27.
[104] Kenneth Frampton, "Introduction: Reflections on the Scope of the Tectonic", *Studies in tectonic culture: the poetics of construction in nineteenth and twentieth century architecture*, Cambridge, Mass.: MIT Press, 1995, p19. Frampton makes use of Eduard Sekler's essay "Structure, Construction, and Tectonics" which can be found in Gyorgy

Kepes (ed.), *Structure in Art and Science*, New York: Braziller, 1965, pp89-95.
[105] For a recent account of ontology and construction, see Gevork Hartoonian, *Ontology of construction: on nihilism of technology in theories of modern architecture*, Cambridge: Cambridge University Press, 1994.

Within the selection of architects featured in this book, Brit Andresen and Peter O'Gorman, Stutchbury and Pape, and Troppo continue to refine this way of making and its associated honesty. Careful attention to the construction joint, and careful framing, both structurally and in terms of placement on the site, inform these works. The palette is almost always exposed light timber and/or steel framing with infills or cladding of sheet fibre cement or corrugated iron. The aesthetic resolution of these houses depends to a large degree on a hierarchy of craftsmanship, from the most pragmatic buildability concerns of Troppo to the exquisite crafted detail of Stutchbury and Pape's Bay House at Watsons Bay, Sydney. The treatment of space is predicated on a climatic condition where the frame can virtually stand alone as the sole spatial delineator, and the roof becomes one of the most fundamental elements of aesthetic expression.

To a lesser degree, the works of Donovan Hill, Sean Godsell, and John Wardle also follow this path, although the notion of the tectonic is less readily applied to how the building stands up, than as to how it might be sheathed or space contained. There is an interest in how a surface is knitted together or cut, with careful attention to detail as if the surface is a piece of joinery. This is a process akin to the weaving of a fabric, or the delicate construction of a screen.[106] It is a different notion of tectonic. Timber is the dominant material of choice, and in larger projects, reinforced concrete is deployed and the expression of panel and joint is explored.

LEVELS OF ABSTRACTION

ANZ Bank (previously ES & A).
Canberra, ACT. 1961. Architect - Stuart McIntosh

Removed from the tradition of visibly articulating the means of making, are those design methods concerned with levels of abstraction, of removing or excising the means of making from the eye, and encouraging sensual reverie within the forms themselves. This has been Harry Seidler's constant quest since his arrival in Australia in 1947, from the completion of his parents' house at Wahroonga, Sydney (1950), to the monumentally dramatic Horizon Apartments, Kings Cross, Sydney (1999). Stuart McIntosh's designs for the ES&A Bank in the late 1950s around Australia were similarly a remarkable series of sculptural forms which derived from McIntosh's experiments with surrealist design techniques.[107] At Heide II, Bulleen, Melbourne (1968), David McGlashan (McGlashan & Everist) designed a house that was a Mondrian maze in the garden for art patrons John and Sunday Reed. Constructed of white Mt Gambier limestone and left to weather, this was live-in abstract sculpture.[108] While it may seem strange to connect them, the same themes of intense formalism can be seen in the neo-Georgian works of Guilford Bell (1912-92)[109], and the subsequent typological

[106] This interest in the screen or woven wall is developed by 19th century German theorist, Gottfried Semper, see Kenneth Frampton, *Studies in tectonic culture: the poetics of construction in nineteenth and twentieth century architecture*, Cambridge, Mass.: MIT Press, 1995, pp84-91. For the definitive account of Semper's ideas, see Harry Francis Mallgrave, *Gottfried Semper: architect of the nineteenth century: a personal and intellectual biography*, New Haven, CT: Yale University Press, 1996.
[107] Stuart McIntosh, "Technique for Design Ideas", *Architecture Today*, February 1960, pp15-17.
[108] Neil Clerehan, "Heide II", *Art in Australia*, September 1968, pp139-141.
[109] L. Van Schaik (ed.), *The life work of Guilford Bell, architect 1912-1992*, Melbourne: Bookman Press, 1999.

consistencies of Alex Tzannes and Alex Popov, and in the sculptural forms of Durbach Block, Ivan Rijavec, and Tom Kovac.[110] The same may be observed in the work of Denton Corker Marshall - at one level, their work in the last ten years approaches a graphic quality, almost two-dimensional in its rigorous formal reduction. At another level, it acknowledges the contemporary state of building practice where cladding buildings in repetitive standardised panel systems makes eminent economic sense.[111]

The Modernist project of abstraction is not pursued just for its seductive visual ends. There is a serious aim beyond the pleasurable (and it is commonly this rather than the grotesque hence sublime), namely that of awakening the body to a sensitised state of spatial and material awareness. For Engelen Moore, there is the goal of a universal mass-produced article within which unadulterated personal expression might be possible. For Kerstin Thompson, abstraction is intended primarily to heighten the awareness of the space shaped without, or the volume shaped within. Each volume becomes its own sculpted landscape. Wood Marsh, by contrast, are excited by the opportunity that architecture might have the same qualities as pieces of

Museum of Modern Art at Heide. Bulleen, Vic. 1968. Architect - McGlashan and Everist

abstract or minimalist modern art, and that they might be used and inhabited at the same time. For Wood Marsh, architecture is occupiable art, and the boundaries between are not obvious. Nation Fender Katsalidis occupy a similar position, but the treatment of form is decidedly more vigorous in expression, almost collagic. In their practice is the critical acknowledgment of the weathering process of materials, and that the city is a family of robustly modelled sculptures - the task is adding to the family.

THE FIGURATIVE

The third path is that of the consciously figurative, a path followed by 1940s painters like Sidney Nolan, Albert Tucker and Arthur Boyd. Their paintings did not reject the human figure, but revelled critically in the representation of national imagery and mythology, and in the mysteriousness of the Australian

[110] See Harry Margalit, *Durbach Block: the luminous space of abstraction*, Sydney, NSW: Pesaro Publishing, 1999; Stephen Crafti (ed.), *House Design: Ivan Rijavec: Pure Form*, Mulgrave, Victoria: Images (Australia), 2000; and Leon Van Schaik (ed.), *Tom Kovac*, London: Academy Editions, 1998.

[111] Philip Goad, "Reinventing Typologies: the Melbourne Exhibition Centre", *UME*, 2 1996, pp28-29.

[112] For accounts of this period of Australian painting, see Richard Haese, *Rebels and precursors : the revolutionary years of Australian art*, Ringwood, Vic.: Allen Lane, 1981; and *Angry Penguins and Realist painting in Melbourne in the 1940s*, Melbourne: Australian Exhibitions Touring Agency, c1989.

by the cloak of minimalism. This approach was mirrored by Melbourne architect Roy Grounds[113], and subsequently by Edmond and Corrigan with their defiant defence of the ordinary architecture of the suburbs. They have contemporary confreres in Ashton Raggatt McDougall (ARM) and Lyons Architects. In one sense, it is no surprise given the obsession with artifice and the visual in the southern capital, where climate has little influence on the culture.

A crucial difference from the socially concerned work of Edmond and Corrigan, and the referential, sometimes effete East/West fusion of Grounds' later works, is the role that digital technology plays in the process of image manipulation and invention. In the case of ARM, they picture buildings. Postwar architectural masterpieces are put through the digital wringer: Aalto's Finlandia Hall, the Vanna Venturi House, Philip Johnson's Glass House, Mitchell Giurgola Thorp's Australian Parliament House, the Villa Savoye, the Sydney Opera House, and Daniel Libeskind's Jewish Museum in Berlin, are put on the rack, stretched, mimicked and venerated. Like Picasso's transformations in paint of Velasquez' ladies of the Spanish court, ARM prod and probe the icons, and test the limits of architectural language.[114] It is a practice unseen anywhere else in the world. Lyons, on the other hand, build pictures. A baby's face is built in bricks, clouds become windows against a sky of metal cladding, the slice through geological strata becomes brick, a large screen (pictured) duplicates Hans Scharoun's Berlin National Library, a huge tyre tread becomes a light filtering façade. Lyons' work moves on from the early work of Robert Venturi into an entirely different realm. It references the work of Japanese architect Kazuo Shinohara amongst others, and without fear, it contends that a wafer-thin surface might be just as revealing as the eternal truths of making.

Box Hill Institute of TAFE. Whitehorse Campus, VIC. 2001. Architect - Lyons

These traditions are not the exclusive domains of the fourteen architects featured in this book. Nor are those individual traditions the only ones adopted by a firm. Some practise in a variety of idioms, and merge one interest with another. Larger offices like Jones Coulter Young and Tonkin Zulaikha Greer cut across the compositional boundaries. Robin Boyd himself was the most direct example of an architect able to slip between compositional traditions. These three traditions can be now distinguished and elaborated upon with a measure of historical pedigree, from the basis of a postwar understanding of space and time.

[113] Philip Goad, "An Oriental Palazzo: Roy Grounds and the National Gallery of Victoria", *Backlogue: Journal of the Halftime Club,* vol.3, 1999, pp73-105.
[114] For various accounts of the design methods of the ARM office, see Harriet Edquist, "Howard Raggatt's 'Critical Architecture': Redeeming the Modern", *Transition,* 21 1987/ Peter Gibson, Alex Lawlor, Peter Brew, "Raiders of the Lost Institution", *Transition,* 27/28 (1989); Howard Raggatt, "Not Vanna Venturi House", *Pataphysics,* 1991; Ian McDougall,

"Dispersion and the Encyclopaedic: Towards New Techniques for the City", *Backlogue: Journal of the Half Time Club,* vol.1, 1992, pp34-41; Ashton Raggatt McDougall, "5 projects, Ashton Raggatt McDougall", *Backlogue: Journal of the Halftime Club,* vol.1, 1992; Richard Munday, "The Emergence of a Difficult Architecture: ... better our work unfinished than all bad", *Backlogue: Journal of the Half time Club,* vol.1, 1992, pp 142-153; Howard Raggatt, " 'Notness', Fin de Siècle and the twenty-first century", *38 South,*

1993; Howard RAGGATT, "The Zone of the Blur", *Transition,* 41, 1993; Geoffrey London, "Ashton Raggatt McDougall: Are they serious or flip?", *Architecture Australia,* 82:2 March 1993; Howard Raggatt, "Not Songs", *Transition,* 44/45 1994; Peter Kohane, "Ashton Raggatt and McDougall's imitative architecture: real and imaginary paths through Storey Hall", *Transition,* 51/2 1996, pp8-15; John Macarthur, "Australian Baroque", *Architecture Australia,* 90:2 March April 2001, pp48-61.

NEGATION AND AFFIRMATION

*In nationalist representations, the colonial experience
of becoming modern is haunted by the fear of
looking unoriginal...*

Dipesh Chakrabarty, *The Difference - Deferral of a Colonial Modernity* [115]

In 19th century Australia, there were alternate hopes and fears of a "marsupial architecture", a local hybrid that might be judged by some as original, and by others as peculiar. In the latter case, international canons of taste might not be to applied to the strangeness of the forms. In some recent work it may be argued that such a situation has come to pass. Yet today, the tensions that emanate from the conflict between polarised tastes of international modern art and deliberately parochial interests underpin the richness of the new directions in Australian architecture. There is the acknowledgment of global participation within an international conversation. In reality though, much Australian practice is of an equally reflexive stance. There is a deliberate search, not for the pedigree of international authenticity, but for the idiosyncratic and inventive, the "savage and scarlet".[116]

If one was to be truly critical, the search for an original architecture is analogous to the extreme individualism of Australian society and politics. In literary and artistic circles, resistance to the ideas of a school or a movement is strong. Such notions of collegiate artistic practice are historically difficult arguments to sustain. The Australian "tall poppy" syndrome, of cutting down star performers to size, is rife within Australia, although outside Australia, former local enemies line up to defend "our Kylie"

[115] Dipesh Chakrabarty, "The Difference – Deferral of a Colonial Modernity", in Frederick Cooper and Laura Stoler (eds), *Tensions of Empire: Colonial Cultures in a Bourgeois World*, Berkeley: University of California Press, 1997, p373. [116] From *Australia* 1939, AD Hope, *Collected Poems, 1930-1965*, Sydney: Angus and Robertson, 1966.

Stanhill Apartments. Melbourne, Vic. 1945-50.
Architect - Romberg and Shaw

Academy of Science. Canberra, ACT. 1959.
Architect - Roy Grounds

or "our Nicole". Fierce pride has meant a culture of competition, and one of simmering criticism that is healthy and intense.

In architecture, that heightened sense of creative autonomy is so pervasive that a theoretical or social commitment to the greater collective presence of the city, or to the urbs of the suburb, is hard to find. The humility, or even at times non-demonstrative position, of Tonkin Zulaikha Greer is positively rare. To work quietly as an interventionist within the city is subtle, rather than polemical.[117] Their position is quiet, less confronting, and their work affirms the greater context of the city. By contrast, Ashton Raggatt McDougall's Museum of Australia, Canberra (2001), is a consciously symbolic signature upon the landscape, and a declaration of Australian identity in its external image. Since its completion, the building has been criticized for its challenge to the perceived unity of language in Canberra. But this negation of the conventional practice of viewing Canberra is contradicted by the architects' clear understanding of the uniqueness of the site on the Acton Peninsula, and the integration of their building with the topography of Canberra. Ashton Raggatt McDougall would argue that this is how the Griffins would have responded to the site. One cannot draw conclusions about a single firm too swiftly. Part of the success of Ashton Raggatt McDougall's Storey Hall is its urban fit within the dense street hugging facades of Swanston Street, Melbourne.[118] Despite the unparalleled visual contrast of the building's representational elements, the overall form and massing is an excellent example of responsible urban design.

The Australian practice of producing 'marsupial' or hybrid designs that confound international tastemakers is not new. Frederick Romberg's Stanhill Apartments, Melbourne (1945-50), were an extraordinary compilation of tributes to modern architectures that in their final form become intrinsically local.[119] Roy Grounds' Australian Academy of Science in Canberra (1959), would appear to be the morphing of two Eero Saarinen buildings at Boston's MIT: the shell forms of the Kresge Auditorium (1955), and the jewel-like moated cylinder of the Kresge Chapel (1955). The same could be said of Donovan Hill's Neville Bonner Building, Brisbane (1999), for its tribute both to the tectonic richness of James Birrell's 1960s buildings in that city and to Italian architect Carlo Scarpa's attention to detail and diminutive set pieces of monumental placemaking. Engelen Moore's Rose House at Kiama, NSW (2000), could be seen as a tribute to the visor-like form of Harry Seidler's Landau House, Whale Beach, Sydney (1952), merged with the modularity and rigour of a Craig Ellwood house as reinterpreted by Glenn Murcutt. Although many of these architects

[117] There is a range of Australian architects whose works exhibit this manner. They include: in Sydney, Alex Tzannes, Alex Popov, and Espie Dods; in Melbourne, the houses of Allan Powell and the institutional buildings of Peter Elliott and Peter Crone.

[118] Storey Hall, its urban fit, and its appreciation by Charles Jencks are discussed by Paul Walker in "Radar Event", *Architecture Australia*, 90.3 May/June 2001, p38.
[119] Conrad Hamann, "Frederick Romberg and the Problem of European Authenticity", in

Roger Butler (ed.), *The Europeans: Émigré artists in Australia 1930-1960*, Canberra: National Gallery of Australia, 1997, pp37-58.

would deny hybridity as a conscious technique, it is a syncretic act that has a basis of differing levels of source and inspiration. It is an oscillation between local and global concerns that pursues the project of modernity, within a qualified stance. Contingency is a current cultural condition.

Wickham Terrace Carpark. Brisbane, Qld. 1961. Architect - James Birrell

Such ideas are in many respects the antithesis of other ideas pursued by architects in this book. In their work, the consonance between architecture, the elements, and landscape is seen as the primary and achievable ideal. Reference and compositional artifice based on traditions and the invention of form are in effect secondary to environmental concerns. A pragmatic functionalism becomes a core basis to each design, and to a large degree, this position has unconsciously acquired for itself a visual tag of identity, even Australian identity. For most of these architects, the additional theme of ecological sustainability has become an overriding ethical and technical question. In the houses and institutional buildings of Troppo, Jones Coulter Young, Brit Andresen and Peter O'Gorman, and Stutchbury and Pape, the questions of natural ventilation, sun-shading, embodied energy, and self-sustaining energy supply and recycled water reticulation become rational and formal directives. Many institutions, like Deakin University in Victoria,

Neville Bonner Building. Brisbane, Qld. 1999. Architect - Donovan Hill with Davenport Campbell and Powell Dods Thorpe

have such technical requirements as a compulsory aspect of any new building commission. Wood Marsh's highly sculpted buildings at Deakin University's Burwood campus follow stringent environmental guidelines. Likewise, all the buildings for the 2000 Olympic Games were subject to strict environmental audits - the cantilevered canopies of Tonkin Zulaikha's lighting pylons on the Olympic Boulevard at Homebush Bay, act both as power generators and shade structures. Yet environmental concerns are not always so explicit or visually emphatic. Donovan Hill's houses are 'breathing' timber boxes, not obviously 'green' in image, and Engelen Moore's houses and apartments are carefully planned, shaded, and fenestrated to allow cross-ventilation and natural convection.

The meeting of environmental concerns and architecture is an ideal sought by all the architects discussed in this book, though each arrive at a solution by different means and with varying degrees of intensity. Of course, there are crossovers between the two positions, and it is incorrect to privilege one position above the other. A comparison of extremes can be found in most countries around the world, however in Australian architecture, that notion of extremities is underacknowledged in the face of the selective gaze of international opinion. It is really then a question of who selects which image to market the country. Identity is thus a troubled but necessary pursuit.

COMING IN FROM THE VERANDAH

As often happens in the approach to an Australian country house, it was difficult to decide where to breach the Lushington homestead. There were verandas, porches, lights, snatches of piano music, whingeing dogs, skittering cats, archways armed with rose thorns, a drift of kitchen smells, but never any real indication of how to enter. Australian country architecture is in some sense a material extension of the contradictory beings who have evolved its elaborate informality, as well as a warning to those who do not belong inside the labyrinth.

Patrick White, *The Twyborn Affair* [120]

In 1999, Australia did not become a republic. In 2001, its major public company, BHP, merged with the multi-national mining giant Billiton. Previously fully government-owned banks, power, and telephone companies have been steadily privatised. The universities are competing for private monies. The largest homebuilder is not the government, but private enterprise. Only two of the six state and two territories have government architects and associated public works departments. The practice of architecture in Australia is now essentially a private enterprise. All of this is accompanied by a new technological revolution based on digital communications and global economics. Today's modernity has a different basis – hence the recently vaunted notion of a "Second Modernity".[121] Yet in Australia, the persuasive arguments for capitulating to such an idea can at least be tempered. Australia's geographical 'tyranny of

[120] Patrick White, *The Twyborn Affair*, Ringwood, Victoria: Penguin, (1979) 1981, p212.
[121] Ulrich Beck, Anthony Giddens, Scott Lash et al, *Reflexive Modernization, Politics,* *Tradition and Aesthetics in the Modern Social Order*, Cambridge: Polity Press in association with Blackwell Publishers, 1994.

distance' and lack of true congestion can be liberating. There is space, freedom to move, to practice in a variety of conditions and for a variety of different people. Yet it is now time to come in from the verandah, to realise the options in front of Australian architecture and perceive the new direction as an architecture culture uniquely poised to ponder its choices.

But if we take the typical form as that surrounding the building on three or four sides, then it is more characteristic of Australia than of any other place. .... But the verandah which is embedded in the Australian culture by way of painting, poems and novels, is not necessarily of the typical surrounding form. Tom Roberts painted the verandahs of Bourke Street, and Russell Drysdale the shop verandahs of country towns. Hal Porter's watcher is on a cast iron balcony, not a verandah in the normal sense at all. It is perhaps because the word 'verandah' is applied to so many different and independent forms that it seems more typical, and more ubiquitous that it really is.[122]

The choice of the phrase "coming in from the verandah" is useful on two counts. Firstly, 'verandah' as somehow being an intrinsic Australian space is acknowledged but questioned. Secondly, the phrase implies that the presence of the verandah is predicated on the simultaneous presence of an inner space. The verandah must surround or be attached to something before it gains its title. One may choose to remain on it, or move to another location. It is an edge condition dependent on other forms of space behind. The same can be said for Australian architecture.

The recent popularisation of the verandah as an intrinsic Australian space[123] is not a new idea. In the 19th century, the virtues of the verandah and the loggia were well expounded and well argued. The covered open-air room still has the potent charge of appropriateness to the place, and being of the place. As Miles Lewis has pointed out, with the historical development of the verandah, such a space is not always strictly speaking, a verandah. Take for instance, Troppo's reinterpretations of its form in the tropical house by bringing the verandah inside, bringing the decking within the perimeter of the house line. Or consider Donovan Hill's monumentalisation of the internal 'outdoor' volumes in many of their houses. The frame-like protrusions of Engelen Moore's Grid Apartments, or even the giant double height opening of their Price O'Reilly House, can be seen as alternative 'verandahs'. These are all examples of designing semi-enclosed outdoor space, and the overriding concern is to provide another reading or refinement of the literal idea of the verandah. Much of the invention of Australian architecture concerns the preoccupation with trying to find an appropriate balance in the provision of such a space.

The second notion of coming in from the verandah is to literally make that analogy. One can take

[122] Miles Lewis, "The Australian Verandah", *Tirra Lirra*, 7: 4 Winter 1997, pp23-24.
[123] Philip Drew, *Veranda: embracing place*, Pymble, N.S.W: Angus & Robertson, 1992.

another position, or several positions, as a possible vehicle for exploration and expression in architecture. This is the key idea behind the new directions in Australian architecture outlined in this book. Ten themes appear and reappear in various forms through the work of the architects featured in this book. These themes lie at the heart of the continuing and irresistible rise of the nation-city, ensuring the maintenance of diversity 'down under' through urban traditions engendered by distinct educational, cultural and geographical differences. Australia's archipelago of architecture cultures nurtures the development of these ten partial views:

'City of Fiction' installation, Museum of Contemporary Art. Sydney, NSW. 1999. Architect - Lyons

THE TOURISTIC AND SCENOGRAPHIC VIEW

In certain Australian practices, acknowledgment is made of the scale and generic nature of the late 20th century city. Lyons' proposition that Melbourne could be Houston could be Toronto is based on the premise that consideration of our cities and urbanised peripheries needs to be conditioned by the fleeting scenographic view, at the speed of the motor car, and with the economic expediency of the postcard. Their view of Melbourne pixilated and cast as hundreds of postcards highlights the various state of the common (not necessarily preferred) experience of space as touristic rather than contemplative.

THE PERSISTENT TECTONIC

The so-called functional tradition of Australian architecture persists through the necessary and expedient adoption of lightweight construction. The act of making and the project of the house are critical practices in this regard. As aesthetic tools, the timber and the steel frame, and lightweight cladding such as corrugated iron and translucent fibreglass engender critical decisions in the adoption of a pure methodological position of explicit joints, connections, and taking delight in the materials themselves.

THE INDIGENOUS AS NEW CATEGORY

In the last twenty years, the question of an architecture for indigenous people, an understanding of indigenous readings of the landscape, and the political necessity of coming to terms with a race that had its lands (and many of its children) removed has become a new category of invention and exploration. There must be a recognition of the indigenous as a new category, not just in remote communities and with the education and employment of indigenous architects, but with an influence on major Australian public buildings. It is also essential to acknowledge that the response is not unitary in form or in process. Troppo's work in this book thus represents but one path.

THE DELIBERATE ARTIFICE

A condition of society's expectations of architecture at the beginning of the twenty-first century is the double edged sword of architectural image as cultural commodity. Formal dexterity, the 'unique' or signature building, is a concept that architects know and understand. It has reached a new level as public entertainment. On the one hand, the autonomy of the position which is afforded the architect is positive. Yet on the other hand, in domestic design, the quest for trophy houses begs the perennial question of architectural elitism. The resultant formal dynamism of contemporary Australian architecture may be seen as a constant last-ditch effort to maintain the integrity of design composition, a form of resistance to the mentality and economics of unenlightened real estate speculation.

Eastern Freeway Sound Barriers.
Doncaster, Vic. 1998.
Architect - Wood Marsh

THE PROBLEMATISED LANDSCAPE

The projects in this book represent shifts away from simplistic notions of the Australian landscape. It is not something to be feared or rejected. It can be engaged, respected, and occasionally reconfigured. There is a sense that contemporary Australian architects can now accept its presence through reasoned critique. From proposals for windswept suburban campuses and sculptural freeway walls, to a direct fusion of landscape and architectural ideals affirming engagement with site and prospect, the terrain has become a potential architectural field – no longer the backdrop for a lone object.

THE DENSELY URBANE

The densely urbane condition in the Australian city is now no longer the sole domain of the corporate commercial office. The argument for congestion is accepted. Whether high rise office towers, inner city apartments, or public domain architecture such as footbridges, terraces, and lighting pylons, such projects indicate a resumption of architectural skill at the level of urban design.

THE POSITIVE NEGATION

The practice of negating the centre is a typically post-structuralist position. It is current. In architecture, the notion of a central authority can vary, It can mean the flaunting of convention that can enrich and reveal. Kerstin Thompson's reinforced concrete beach house at Anglesea is not a typical response. Donovan Hill's HH House verges on the monumental, but uses the humble tomato stake. Jones Coulter Young's airport at the remote location of Exmouth is not what one might expect. And it might literally mean the negation of

Australian Institute of Aboriginal and Torres Strait Islander Studies. Canberra, ACT. 2001, Architect - arm.rpvht

globally understood conventions. ARM's painting black the once pure white forms of a Villa Savoye despatched to Canberra is one such case. Such negations need not be seen as arrogant obtuseness but as critical design tactics.

THE PROCESS AS EXPERIMENT

The technological advances in architecture of the last twenty years have not been material or structural, but have been embodied within the design process, especially so in terms of the possibilities of digital technology. The techniques of the computer, which defy the reality of making, can absorb and propose the image as expedient, immediate, and all important. The idea of a post-Euclidean space is possible. In recent Australian architecture, two firms are pre-eminent: ARM and Lyons. Their achievement has been the translation from digital image to built work. The canons of taste are sent packing and the juries remain perplexed.

THE GHOST OF THE SOCIAL

For the most part, no social program is explicit in these current works. The obvious exceptions are John Wardle's projects for the Salvation Army in Melbourne, Sean Godsell's altruistic Future Shack, and Troppo's housing and community-based projects for indigenous communities in the Northern Territory (which form a small part of a much larger and diverse program). The formalist concerns and conscientious investigations of multiple housing types, the intense interest in urban design, and the concentration on buildings for education are a telling reflection of current Australian society. The ghost of the social in architecture is yet to emerge from another cycle of relative affluence in Australian architecture, a period matched by Australia in the late 1950s, the mid-1960s and the late-1980s.

Melbourne Exhibition Centre. Vic. 1996. Architect - Denton Corker Marshall

THE NEW VERANDAH

The persistent search in much of Australian architecture has been the development of the semi-enclosed outdoor space. The term 'verandah' was not always adopted to describe such a space. Many of the architects in this book are intent on discovering a 'new verandah'. It is a search that in its experimental form almost always takes place within the realm of domestic design. Yet in the 19th century, the verandah was defined as a crucial public space within the city.

In the last fifteen years, Mitchell Giurgola Thorp's Great Verandah at Parliament House, Canberra; Peddle Thorp's colonnade at East Circular Quay, Sydney; and Denton Corker Marshall's Exhibition Centre in Melbourne, are the most literal attempts to return such an idea to the public realm.

The seeds of a new verandah may lie in Ashton Raggatt McDougall's Boolean knot of the National Museum of Australia spinning out into the Canberra landscape, Peter Stutchbury's twisted roof for the International Archery Park for Sydney 2000, or perhaps more quietly as a canopy of trees framing an outback schoolroom. The verandah always focuses on the look out, but there is also the reverse view, or the move back in. One is never exclusively present, nor independent of the other. The same must be said of these new directions in contemporary Australian architecture.

ANDRESEN O'GORMAN

Brit Andresen (born Sandnes, Norway, 1945) spent her early childhood and was educated in Sydney, before leaving Australia to study architecture. She graduated from NTH, Trondheim, Norway in 1969. Between 1970 and 1977 she taught and was in sole practice in England. From 1971 to 1976 she also worked in association with Barry Gasson and John Meunier on the Burrell Museum, Glasgow, and in 1977 she returned to Australia. Peter O'Gorman (born Brisbane, 1940) graduated in architecture from The University of Queensland in 1965. From 1965 to 1979 he taught and was in sole practice. Andresen and O'Gorman have practised together since 1980. Andresen has taught at the Cambridge School of Architecture, the Architectural Association (London), University of California, (Los Angeles), and at the University of Queensland. O'Gorman taught design at The University of Queensland from 1968 to 1998. The firm's work has been exhibited in Paris, Milan, Venice, Singapore, and Adelaide. Important completed projects include: Deer Park Sanctuary Lodge, Buderim, Queensland (1980); Mt Nebo House, Queensland (1984); North Stradbroke Island House (1986, with Timothy Hill); Tom's Gateway House, Queensland (1988); Ocean View Farmhouse, Mt Mee, Queensland (1994); Rosebery House, Highgate Hill, Queensland (1998); Mooloomba House, North Stradbroke Island, Queensland (1998); Wynnum Houses, Wynnum, Queensland (2001). The firm's work has been published in numerous books and journals including: *10x10*, London: Phaidon (2000); Paco Asensio, *Mountain Houses*, New York: Loft Publications (2000); *Abitare* (Italy); *Architectural Record* (USA); *A+U* (Japan); and *UME*.

Mooloomba House

ANDRESEN O'GORMAN

Brit Andresen and Peter O'Gorman take their architecture very seriously. They also take their time. Each house they design is a piece of detailed research - a laboratory for three things: refining the use of Australian hardwood as a building material; the use of mathematical proportions and harmonic series as ordering devices; and the constant search for an appropriate creation and definition of place. Binding it all is the notion of a poetics of construction, finding the right material, the right metre, and the right atmosphere or evocation for their site and their client. As full-time educators in architecture at The University of Queensland in Brisbane for more than thirty years, they have had to be patient - building little but building well.

Andresen returned to Australia from England in 1977 after researching the Dutch housing experiments of Bakema and Habraken at Eindhoven, and then teaching and working in Britain from 1970. In 1980, she collaborated with O'Gorman on the design of the Deer Park Sanctuary Lodge at Buderim (1980), north of Brisbane. The central concept was a long gable-roofed public hall with an attached flat-roofed kitchen and amenity block to one side. At the north end, the major gable continued beyond a curving rock fireplace, and externally as a pergola of boldly crossed rafters with a pair of steel antlers at the end of the major beams. The entire

Deer Park Sanctuary Lodge. Buderim, Qld. 1980.

scheme was rigorous and consistent in its modulation, with the saddlebagging of service spaces off the major nave-like volume.

Subsequent houses like the Mt Nebo House, Queensland (1984), and Stradbroke Island House (1986,

with Timothy Hill), demonstrate the dextrous layering of screens and battens, with expressed timber construction typical of the traditional Queensland house. The former was a tower house generated from the geometries of the square (man) and the circle (spirit). The latter comprised additions to and the refurbishment of a 1950s house, utilizing decks as necessary thresholds, connecting with the landscape.

At Mount Mee, the linear form of the Ocean View Farmhouse (1994), followed the hillside contour, and was split by a breezeway deck into a wing of bedrooms, and a self-contained living/main bedroom

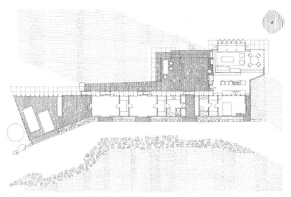

Ocean View Farmhouse plan. Mount Mee, Qld. 1994.

photograph courtesy Andresen O'Gorman

Ocean View Farmhouse. Mount Mee, Qld. 1994.

block that stepped gently down the slope to the view. The south side of the house faced up the hill and was given a protective armature of black timber battens over metal decking, while to the north, the house opens itself out to the landscape. From the guest bedrooms, doors slide to one side, and one steps onto a giant rock and a timber walkway. At the Ormond House, Indooroopilly (1980-91), the parti was similar but the separated pavilion was treated as a tower/sleeping block and telescoped corners became window seats, places to contemplate and savour the view.

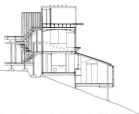

Ormond House section. Indooroopilly, Qld. 1980-91.

Ormond House plan

While these houses demonstrate Andresen O'Gorman's careful orchestration of site, construction and intimately-followed client concerns, three recent domestic projects epitomise the firm's cumulative refinements. They represent a special synthesis of experiential application and spiritual possibility.

On North Stradbroke Island, the Mooloomba House (1998), is Andresen O'Gorman's temple to timber. It reveals O'Gorman's four decades of research into the structural capacities of the fickle Australian hardwood. It also reveals Andresen's long-time interest in Queensland's 19th century timber churches, and reflects the spatial flexibility of old houses in Norway and Japan, where spaces and furniture take on a portable character. Their interest in systems, and the unified endeavour that results in aesthetic pleasure being found in an exposed timber frame is blended with a shared interest in placemaking. Above all is the steadfast belief that there is a poetry of construction consonant with a poetry of dwelling.

Perched on a steep slope above the road, the Mooloomba House is essentially a long inhabited 'wall' with two permanent 'tents' attached. The 'wall' is defined by the extrusion of a 1200mm wide gallery with two 600mm wide spaces cantilevered at the upper level to either side, one being the slimmest of corridors, the other defining bed boxes that hug the east louvred wall. In section, the concept is reminiscent of Palladio's strategic overlaying of classical temples to define a new typology of church. At Mooloomba, one frame is slipped over another, and a gabled roof clad in corrugated fibre cement is slung over the top. The framing members are built up of paired tiny hardwood sections bolted together - the grains are opposed to counteract warping - with plywood filler. Stained with black pigment, the final impression and the structural capability of these timber members is like black steel. One of the 'tents' is an open dining space defined by an aedicule of four cypress logs, enclosed by an inner lining of battens and an outer lining of translucent fibreglass. The other 'tent' is a living space also defined by log poles, and both look onto a sand-floor court which contains its own forest of log poles. This western side of the house, alternately open and closed beneath simple skillion roofs, represents the ideal of living beneath the most fundamental of natural shelters (the tree), while the adjacent overlaid series of frames that forms the gabled container signifies the next cultural step (the hut).

The two-level four bedroom Rosebery House (1998), is located in Highgate Hill on a steep slope running down to the Brisbane River. Entry is across a creek gully, and one

Mooloomba House. North Stradbroke Island, Qld. 1998.

is confronted by a great wall of battens, a virtual forest of sticks. One passes through this filigree layer onto a timber deck, before ascending to a sliding spine of alternately open and closed living and sleeping spaces. Overhead and underfoot, there are timber battens. The major structural members are stained black, yet other black members defy a purely structural reading. The walls and roof become a syncopated rhythm of lines, and the glazing is divided horizontally into clear and milky leadlight sections by a mathematical series. To live in this house is to live in a magical timber frame, half inside and half out, continually dappled with striated shade.

At Wynnum, on Moreton Bay in suburban Brisbane, Andresen O'Gorman have designed two structures (2001), side by side on separate titles. Originally intended for a community of four single independent women who might share facilities, zoning regulations only permitted one 'house' per site, so the solution was to build two houses with the potential for use as four self-contained apartments. Using familiar themes of an exposed post and beam structure, with twinned hardwood posts on either side of a plywood panel, the aim was to make a tranquil contemplative paradise on a constricted site. Shelter was made from Andresen O'Gorman's notion of 'inwoven shade.' One lives within a giant trellis, or pergola. Each opening into the central courtyard space is defined by folding panel doors or sliding *shoji* screens, and the impression is one of a serene Japanese house. Studied proportions, carefully orchestrated visual axes, and adjustable transparency suggest new ways of living in sub-tropical Australia. This scheme is perfectly poised for Brit Andresen and Peter O'Gorman's next venture into the refinement of the essential nature of dwelling.

MOOLOOMBA HOUSE

ANDRESEN O'GORMAN

1st floor

MOOLOOMBA HOUSE | North Stradbroke Island | Queensland | 1998

ground floor

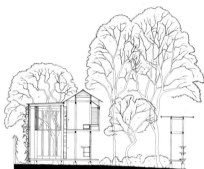

section

east elevation

ground floor plan

1st floor plan

MOOLOOMBA HOUSE | North Stradbroke Island | Queensland | 1998

ROSEBERY HOUSE

ANDRESEN O'GORMAN

west elevation

ROSEBERY HOUSE | Highgate Hill | Queensland | 1998

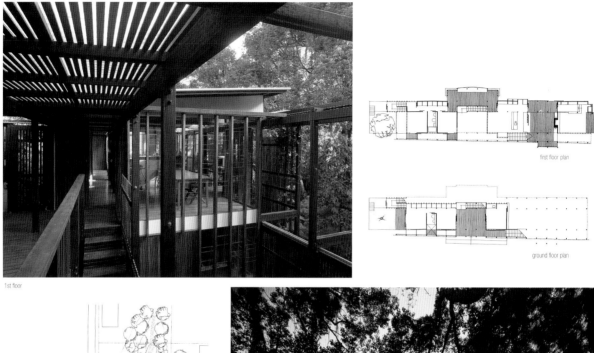

first floor plan

ground floor plan

1st floor

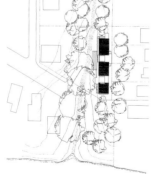

site plan

west elevation

ROSEBERY HOUSE | Highgate Hill | Queensland | **1998**

ANDRESEN O'GORMAN

ROSEBERY HOUSE | Highgate Hill | Queensland | **1998**

WYNNUM HOUSES

ANDRESEN O'GORMAN

west elevation

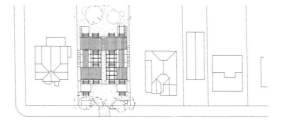

WYNNUM HOUSES | Wynnum | Queensland | **2001**

south house

WYNNUM HOUSES | Wynnum | Queensland | **2001**

ANDRESEN O'GORMAN

north house 1st floor

south house

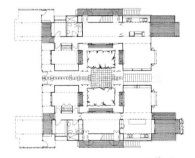

1st floor plan

ground floor plan

courtyard from north house

ASHTON RAGGATT MCDOUGALL

Stephen Ashton (born Sydney, 1954) graduated in architecture from The University of Melbourne in 1977. From 1977-82 he worked for Daryl Jackson Evan Walker Pty Ltd, Peter Sanders, and Max May. Howard Raggatt (born Melbourne, 1951) graduated from The University of Melbourne in 1978 and worked for Norman Day from 1979 to 1981. The firm of Ashton and Raggatt was established in 1984. Ian McDougall (born Gawler, South Australia, 1952) graduated from Royal Melbourne Institute of Technology in 1979. Between 1976 and 1980, he worked for Max May, Kevin Borland, Peter Crone, and Edmond & Corrigan. From 1983-86, McDougall was a director of the MMH Partnership. In 1979, McDougall was co-founder and editor (with Richard Munday) of the critical journal Transition. The firm of Ashton Raggatt McDougall was established in 1988. Raggatt and McDougall gained their Masters of Architecture from RMIT University in 1992 and 1994 respectively. Both are Adjunct Professors at RMIT University. Important completed projects include: St Kilda Town Hall Redevelopment and Library Extensions, St Kilda, Victoria (1994); Promedicus Medical Centre, Richmond, Victoria (1995); Storey Hall, RMIT, Melbourne, Victoria (1995); National Museum of Australia, Canberra, Australian Capital Territory (2001, in association with Robert Peck Von Hartel Trethowan). The firm's work has appeared in *Fin de Siecle and the twenty-first century*, Melbourne: RMIT (1993); Leon van Schaik (ed.), *Transfiguring the Ordinary*, Melbourne: Printed Books (1995); Charles Jencks, The *Architecture of the Jumping Universe*, London: Academy Editions (1997); *10x10*, London: Phaidon (2000); *Domus* (Italy); *Architectural Design* (UK); and *Blueprint* (UK).

National Museum of Australia

ASHTON RAGGATT MCDOUGALL

The architecture of Melbourne-based Ashton Raggatt McDougall (ARM) is like no other in Australia. It may have no counterpart anywhere in the world. It is a critical architecture, and intensely cerebral. The work does not concern itself with orthodox notions of architectural space, linguistic conventions or tectonic truths. ARM actively distance themselves from commitment to a single aesthetic, and conventional architectural 'taste'. Their work is emphatically edgy with its direct borrowing and manipulation of known imagery. Their aim is a discursive architecture, an architecture that challenges the mind and the body, brimming with content and restless with ideas.

Early signs of subverting convention were shown in 1980s exhibition pieces by Howard Raggatt, and with the Drummond Street offices, Carlton, Victoria (1986), by Ashton & Raggatt. This building was a collage of tilt-slab concrete, brick veneer, mirrored glass curtain wall, pebble-tex, and faux bolt heads. At the building's corner, one isn't sure which pieces are really necessary and which elements are ornamental, and it is this uncertainty that others find disturbing. When Ian McDougall joined Ashton and Raggatt in 1988 to form ARM, he brought a strong interest in architectural history, and the conviction that historical time was irrelevant, due to the pluralistic and encyclopaedic range of architectural language. The Brunswick Community Health Care Centre, Brunswick, Victoria (1990), drew from the innovative program of McDougall's Kensington Community Health Care Centre, Kensington, Victoria (1985). ARM mined the architectural imagery of the surroundings as a means of direct identification with the place. Two scaled-up bay windows, a warehouse shed (about to turn into a high rise building), and a tilt-slab speculative office building were amalgamated, cheek by jowl, into a literally compacted street façade.

Drummond Street offices. Carlton, Vic. 1986.

Community Health Care Centre. Brunswick, Vic. 1990.

At the Kronborg Medical Clinic, Footscray, Victoria (1992), ARM shifted into an altogether more sophisticated *modus operandi*, a process driven by the computer, and by Howard Raggatt's theory of 'Notness'. Iconic pieces of modern architecture could be probed and prodded, their formal limits tested by direct quotation and digital manipulation. The aim was that through transfiguration, transformation (visual, sensual and spiritual) might take place. The operation would be cathartic, so as to release the 'icon' to develop new meanings and new contexts. Such a process not only acknowledged the 'death of the author', it signified commitment to digital design as a 'cultural leap into the unknown'. Thus an image of Robert Venturi's Vanna Venturi House, Philadelphia, USA (1962), a postmodern 'icon', was dragged through a photocopier, stretched, pixilated, distorted, and constructed directly from the stretch. At the St Kilda Town Hall Redevelopment, St Kilda, Victoria (1994), Alvar Aalto's Finlandia Hall was shrunk and reproduced as a rear façade to council offices, and its volumetric reverse became an internal baroque public thoroughfare between old and new. At the same time across the street, ARM added a giant open stone book with a picture window to Enrico Taglietti's

St. Kilda Public Library (1969). At the Promedicus Medical Centre, Richmond, Victoria (1995), the west wall was formed by the impression of an invisible Fuller geodesic dome. The certainties of science were borrowed for the inverse of their original effect. What should be a controlled environment inside the dome is actually outside it. These design processes are much more than simply radical eclecticism - newness comes from the conceit of the simultaneously 'automatic' and 'unknown' process of digital manipulation. These are concoctions that cannot be imagined, they can only be found by swirling the beakers of virtual space.

Federation Square competition entry. 1997.

Singapore Management University competition entry. 2000.

Trackside development proposal. City of Moreland. Vic. 2001.

Storey Hall and Annexe, RMIT University, Melbourne, Victoria (1995), is coloured a vivid green in honour of the Hibernian Irish Catholic Community who built the original 1887 hall, combined with purple and white, the colours of the Women's Political Association (formed in 1916). The building is devotional - fragments of much loved Melbourne monuments such as the Griffins' Capitol Theatre ceiling and sculptor Ron Robertson-Swann's canary yellow Vault appear in the upper level foyer and the auditorium. Mathematician Roger Penrose's deliberations on the pentagon are given expressionistic range in the auditorium ceiling, along with a recollection of Buckminster Fuller's folded map of the world in triangles. A bay window projects over Swanston St through weathered green metal panels embossed with lacy suspender belts and the words 'Resurrection City'. These panels appear like the foliage of trees above a grotto-like entry, with a tomb-like slab of timber as a bench seat. This cave in the garden hints at a most profound layer of embodied meaning.

ARM proclaim that 'architects do more than just houses' and that they would prefer to leave tastemaking to others. Décor is not beyond them though, and in the redesign of the subterranean interior of the Amcor Lounge (1996), at the Victorian Arts Centre, they produced dazzling backlit perspex murals. Plastic spiders, marbles, rings, baubles, and even a pair of handcuffs are embedded in the perspex. As one arrives and leaves, mirrors distort the body - transformation again is the message. The Federation Square competition entry (1997), saw the emergence of a spectacular looping string, a metaphorical knot, seen against the background of the Melbourne city centre. Another competition entry, for the Singapore Management University (2000), evinced a further elaboration of a looping knotted string, diving in and out of the campus like a giant earthworm. The Marion Cultural Centre in suburban Adelaide (2000- in association with Philips Pilkington), comprises a diverse community of buildings, furthering ARM's notion of "intense adjacencies" enhanced by different plays of scale and proportional disruption. Historical referencing, incongruity, and suburban affirmation are keyed into Trackside, a proposal for apartment towers in the flat northern suburbs of Melbourne. Referencing the "skyhook" schemes of El Lissitzky, these towers will provide a "Collectivist gateway", a suburban periscope from which citizens can view the city in the distance.

Such confounding of expectations is explored to the full in ARM's most controversial building to date, the National Museum of Australia (NMA) on the Acton Peninsula, Canberra, ACT (2001). There, in association with Robert Peck von Hartel Trethowan, ARM realised their explorations of linguistic 'nots' and physical 'knots'. The NMA tangles the Griffins' axes of urban democracy, acknowledges that the popular culture of the museum is now a surrogate for what modern art can no longer say on a gallery wall, and the complex rhetoric of the knot hints at the misunderstood material and spiritual culture of Australia's indigenous people. The Museum's entry, its circulation, the Gehry-esque forms of its Great Hall and the captured views to Canberra's landmarks are all determined by the knotting, looping, and intertwining trajectory of a hollow Boolean string of pentagonal section. One begins the journey underneath a luminous pentagon, and from there the steel-sheeted forms describe a baroque spatial sequence. The massive rusted forms of Clement Meadmore and the sculptures of Claes Oldenburg.are recalled. Fragments and details of James Stirling's Neue Staatsgalerie in Stuttgart, glazing from the Sydney Opera House, and the zig-zagging forms of Daniel Libeskind's Jewish Museum in Berlin, are literally strung together. The string and its knots underpin the whole scheme. The reference to 19th century German architectural theorist Gottfried Semper's proposition that the knot was one of the first pieces of symbolic human artifice resonates as a monument to indigenous Australians. It is both a celebration and a shaming of the colonial project, and a tribute to the diversity of contemporary Australian culture. The Garden of Australian Dreams (GOAD), designed by landscape architects Room 4.1.3., is a dazzling piece of landscape art - a 3D Pop Art street directory of an 'other' Australia, undulating and tattooed with lines, streets, and fences, with indigenous and European place names. Leading away from it is a new axis, the Uluru line, which points to a different centre, and terminates on the ground in a reflexive curl. The crescent shape of the Museum is like a coiled snake, and when the Boolean string emerges from the interior, the gold and bronze panelled skin is scarred red with pointed head ('European') windows. The skin has two sets of writing on it. One is a series of fragments of the word 'Eternity', etched into Australia's consciousness on the footpaths of Sydney by Arthur Stace. The other is giant braille that only a blind God can read. The Museum is adjoined by the Australian Institute of Aboriginal and Torres Strait Islander Studies, featuring a black Villa Savoye, a wry and pointed negation of a "white" icon.

ARM's subversive tactics are aimed at the autonomous aspect of the discipline of architecture, and argue that meaning as represented by architectural form has a continuing role in contemporary culture. They probe the very pieces of architecture and the way in which they go together, how these pieces of architecture are conceived, and of how they engage their own hold over fashion and convention. ARM do not hold to the sway of post-structural reverence for abstraction, but they are fascinated by the iconic power possessed by internationally famous works of architecture. To think locally is to go directly to such sources and make one's critique. The world is their oyster, but the field and the art of their technique is defiantly local.

ST KILDA LIBRARY

ST KILDA LIBRARY | St Kilda | Victoria | **1994**

ST KILDA TOWN HALL

1st floor plan

ST KILDA TOWN HALL │ St Kilda │ Victoria │ **1994**

STOREY HALL

west elevation

ASHTON RAGGATT MCDOUGALL

STOREY HALL | RMIT University | Melbourne | Victoria | 1996

auditorium ceiling

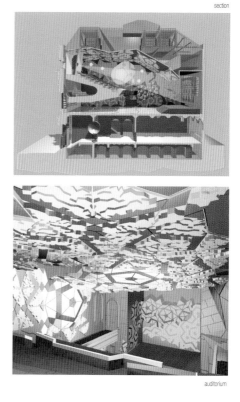

section

auditorium

west elevation

STOREY HALL | RMIT University | Melbourne | Victoria | **1996**

PROMEDICUS

PROMEDICUS | Richmond | Victoria | **1995**

AMCOR LOUNGE
VICTORIAN ARTS CENTRE

THE NATIONAL MUSEUM OF AUSTRALIA

ASHTON RAGGATT MCDOUGALL

permanent gallery west facade

THE NATIONAL MUSEUM OF AUSTRALIA | Canberra | ACT | 2001

as arm.rphvt - a joint venture with Robert Peck von Hartel Trethowan

main hall

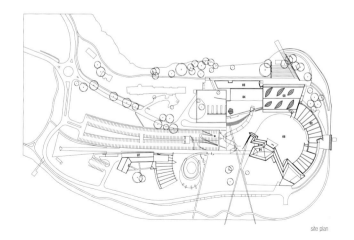

site plan

THE NATIONAL MUSEUM OF AUSTRALIA | Canberra | ACT | **2001**

main entrance looking to permanent gallery

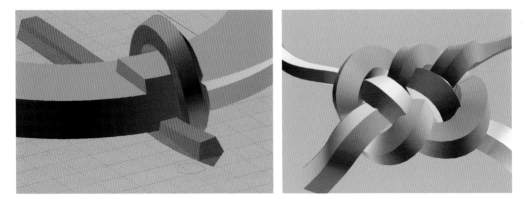

THE NATIONAL MUSEUM OF AUSTRALIA | Canberra | ACT | **2001**

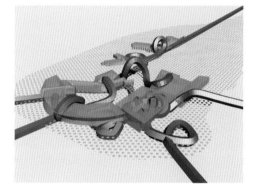

main hall elevation and Garden of Australian Dreams

Garden of Australian Dreams looking south east

THE NATIONAL MUSEUM OF AUSTRALIA | Canberra | ACT | **2001**

ASHTON RAGGATT MCDOUGALL

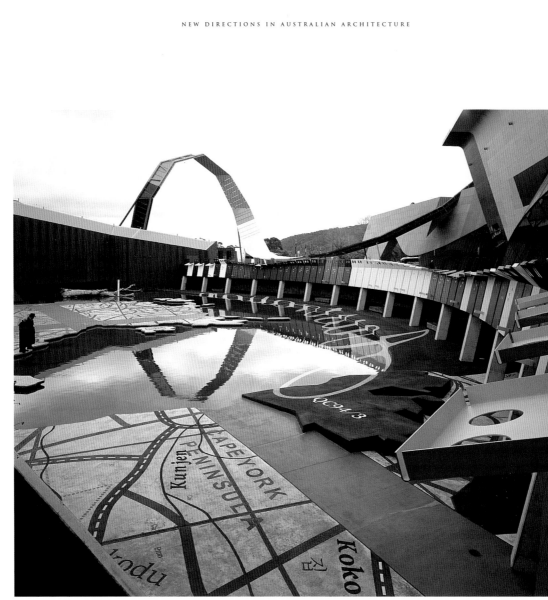

Garden of Australian Dreams looking north west

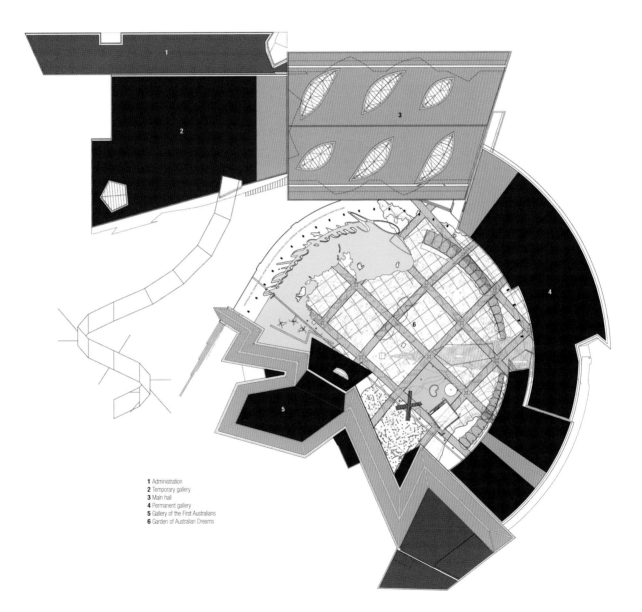

1 Administration
2 Temporary gallery
3 Main hall
4 Permanent gallery
5 Gallery of the First Australians
6 Garden of Australian Dreams

THE NATIONAL MUSEUM OF AUSTRALIA | Canberra | ACT | 2001

DONOVAN HILL

DONOVAN HILL

Brian Donovan (born Emerald, Queensland, 1959) graduated in architecture from The University of Queensland in 1985. After working for Peter O'Gorman in Brisbane, he worked in Japan for Atsushi Kitagawara (1988-89). Timothy Hill (born Brisbane, 1963) graduated in architecture from The University of Queensland in 1990. He worked for Brit Andresen before the partnership of Donovan Hill was established in Brisbane in 1991. Both Donovan and Hill are Adjunct Associate Professors at the University of Queensland. The firm's work has been exhibited in New York, Washington, Paris, Barcelona, Glasgow, Sydney, and Stuttgart. Important completed projects include the HH House, Brisbane, Queensland (1991); T House, Sunshine Coast, Queensland (1994); Neville Bonner Office Building, Brisbane, Queensland (1998, with Davenport Campbell Architects and Powell Dods Thorpe Architects); C House, Brisbane, Queensland (1998); D House, New Farm, Queensland (2000); and AQIS Building, Brisbane Airport, Queensland (2000). The firm's work has appeared in numerous books and journals including *10x10*, London: Phaidon (2000); Clare Melhuish, *Modern House 2*, London: Phaidon (2000); Deyan Sudjic, *Home: the twentieth century house*, London: Laurence King (1999); *Architecture Australia*; and *The Architectural Review* (UK).

Neville Bonner Building

DONOVAN HILL

In Queensland, the architecture of Brian Donovan and Timothy Hill represents the exception rather than the rule. Unlike the previous generation of Rex Addison, Russell Hall, John Mainwaring, and Lindsay and Kerry Clare who reinterpreted the elevated timber Queensland house, and explored the expressive potential of the pitched roof, Donovan Hill's concerns are newly independent. Their work is also substantially divergent from that of architects and educators Brit Andresen and Peter O'Gorman under whom both Donovan and Hill studied and worked, and whose carefully proportioned timber buildings they respect and admire. When the Donovan Hill partnership was formed in 1991, both had a strong interest in timber construction. Donovan worked in Japan for Atsushi Kitawagara (1988-89), where he was made fully aware of the aesthetic economy of contemporary Japanese architecture. Hill worked with Brit Andresen, and detailed a small timber house they had designed on Stradbroke Island, Queensland (1990). From the outset, the buildings of Donovan Hill have had unusual aspirations: monumentality (mass) matched with 'the making of miniatures' through exquisite detail fragments (lightness); the re-inscribing of the entire site as a potential architectural field; and the consistent investigation of a new spatial type for Brisbane's sub-tropical climate - the ventilating and open-air 'significant room' or space, within either a house or an institutional building.

Donovan Hill's first major work was the HH House, Brisbane, Queensland (1991), a low-budget addition to a typical 'Queenslander'. Instead of modest contextual deferral, the response was a heroic hollow façade constructed from the most humble piece of timber, the tomato stake, and roughly poured but heavily modelled off-form concrete. From the rear, the house is a monument to pleasing decay. Weathering, the patina of age, the use of as-found pieces of marble, timber linings from the original house, and a strategy of exaggerating the gaps between things are mixed with a distinctive approach to the arranging of space. Instead of Loos' *raumplan* and its assumption of a hermetic enclosure, Donovan Hill let their volumes 'breathe'.

In the prefabricated timber T House (1994), located behind coastal dunes, the same themes reappear. While the box-like house is tiny, its double height outdoor room is grand, with a seating nest perched within its volume. Donovan Hill operate constantly with scale changes, from the intimate space of children at a built-in seat to a giant framed view of coastal banksias.

The most sophisticated iteration of these ideas occurs in the C House, Brisbane, designed in 1991 and completed in 1998. In a suburban setting, this house is much smaller than it actually appears. The scale is magnified by its 'city square', a 'significant room', which is the largest volume contained by the house. Roofed, but open to the elements, this space can be accessed by all rooms in the house. The other major

DONOVAN HILL

space is the so-called 'Formal Room', a vast entertaining hall that could be the setting for a private opera. When closed off, the remainder of the house can be experienced as an enfilade of intimately scaled spaces, detailed with sliding timber screens, finely crafted joinery, and Scarpa-like inlays of precious coloured tiles and metals. The drama of the house comes not only from the sequential unfolding of the spaces from small to large to small, but also from the material and construction strategy deployed. Concrete was the primary and grounding carcass to the building. This dictated the treatment of the site which was reinscribed as an elaborate landscape of walls, steps, seats, ledges, and at one level, a long narrow pool. The concrete is of exceptional quality. Externally it has been given a layered sedimentary texture. Internally, it is glassy smooth, and in the great central space, stacked layers of local sandstone create more tactile delight. The secondary carcass is timber, used in a myriad of tectonic possibilities, from support to screen to decoration. Exquisite 'baskets' of decks, criss-crossed battens, silky smooth stair treads, and folding shutters can be seen. A woven timber ceiling lining is the final textural layer to this monumental nest.

In a multi-functional teaching workshop for engineering and architecture students at the University of Queensland (1998), Donovan Hill (with associate architect Fedor Medek) have reconfigured an existing embankment as a building that is at once didactic and acutely site responsive. Laminated veneer lumber beams cantilever over bluestone walls, while the new level above the workshop becomes an outdoor teaching space.

Architecture and Engineering Workshop, University of Queensland. Brisbane. 1998.

The robust expression of component structural parts, combined with the aesthetic qualities of repetition is explored with the Neville Bonner Building (1998), designed in collaboration with Davenport Campbell and Powell Dods Thorpe. Echoing the same vigorous modelling employed by James Birrell in Brisbane's institutional and university buildings in the late 1950s and 1960s, Donovan Hill treat each surface according to solar and acoustic orientation. Overlooking the Brisbane River and a multi-deck freeway, the western facade is a symphony of interlocking concrete baffles. Facing the city over a sunken terrace garden is a six level façade of horizontal aluminium sunscreens, and the exterior wall of the block containing the soaring foyer volume is treated as a series of Donovan Hill 'miniatures': a masterpiece of dextrous facade articulation.

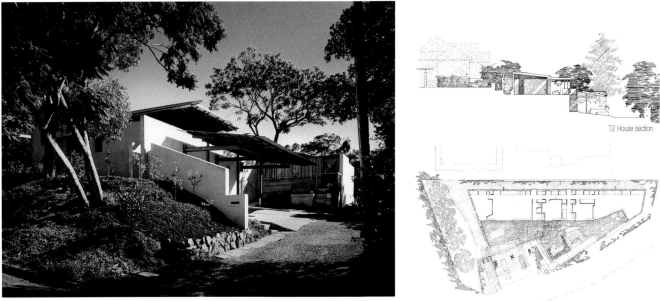

T2 House section

T2 House. Taringa, Qld. 2000.

T2 House site plan

The choice of architectural elements which define a building's presence and stay free from functional change, informs Donovan Hill's AQIS Building at Brisbane Airport (2000). The tough external shell becomes another exploration of intelligent solar treatment. The reduced aesthetic of repetitive baffles, tinted glass, and concrete fin walls engages with the marshy landscape. A building such as this indicates Donovan Hill's willingness to investigate typologies with implications for larger, more repetitive works. With the dual occupancy T2 House at Taringa (2000), and the Clarence Road apartments, Indooroopilly (2001), Donovan Hill explore issues of mass and lightness, and degrees of privacy and transparency applied to multiple dwelling types.

The D House, New Farm, Queensland (2000), suggests possibilities for a medium-density housing type in a suburban setting. Built in the back portion of an existing suburban lot, this modest two bedroom house was developed as if it were the walled garden of the existing house. The 'significant room' is a long roofed terrace, glazed at either end. Bedrooms and service rooms form a thickened wall to the side boundary, and facing the street is an Aaltoesque sliding timber screen. From the built-in timber seat in the living room, one can choose to live either in a totally private courtyard or in a semi-public front garden. As with all Donovan Hill's work, the opening in the wall becomes the crucial filter and the provider of scale. It is the viewing frame, the monumental picture, and a comforting balustrade to the world outside.

HH HOUSE

south facade

HH HOUSE | Brisbane | Queensland | **1991**

HH HOUSE | Brisbane | Queensland | **1991**

T HOUSE

east elevation

1st floor plan

ground floor plan

T HOUSE | Sunshine Coast | Queensland | **1994**

DONOVAN HILL

living room from 1st floor

section

T HOUSE | Sunshine Coast | Queensland | **1994**

C HOUSE

DONOVAN HILL

north east elevation

C HOUSE | Brisbane | Queensland | 1998

view west from 2nd floor

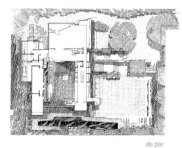

site plan

section

C HOUSE | Brisbane | Queensland | 1998

1st floor

DONOVAN HILL

C HOUSE | Brisbane | Queensland | **1998**

1st floor

C HOUSE | Brisbane | Queensland | **1998**

NEW DIRECTIONS IN AUSTRALIAN ARCHITECTURE

NEVILLE BONNER BUILDING

entry facade and office wing

NEVILLE BONNER BUILDING | Brisbane | Queensland | **1998**
in association with Powell Dods & Thorpe and Davenport Campbell

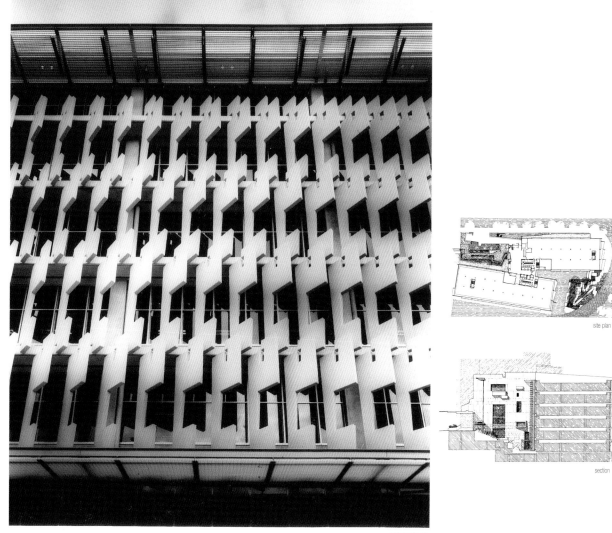

site plan

section

south west facade

AQIS BUILDING

DONOVAN HILL

main block from north east

site plan

north elevation

AQIS BUILDING | Brisbane Airport | Queensland | **2000**

CLARENCE ROAD APARTMENTS

east elevation

site plan

section

NEW DIRECTIONS IN AUSTRALIAN ARCHITECTURE

D HOUSE

west elevation

living room from north

DONOVAN HILL

west elevation

D HOUSE | New Farm | Queensland | 2001

living room from south

site plan

section

ENGELEN MOORE

Ian Moore (born Warkworth, New Zealand, 1958) studied engineering at the Auckland Technical Institute (1976-79) whilst working as a structural engineering technician for Beca Carter Hollings and Ferner in Auckland, New Zealand. From 1980-83, he worked for Ove Arup in Sydney, London, and Hong Kong. Moore moved to Sydney in 1983 and graduated in architecture from the University of Technology, Sydney in 1988. After working for Burley Katon Halliday, Moore established his own office in 1990, and formed Engelen Moore with Tina Engelen in 1995. Engelen (born Melbourne, Australia, 1963) studied interior design at Sydney College of the Arts 1984-1985. She worked for Burley Katon Halliday where she met Ian Moore in 1987, and was then briefly in partnership with designers Marc Newson and Danny Venlet. Moore has taught at The University of Sydney, University of Technology, Sydney, and University of New South Wales. In 2000, he completed his Masters of Architecture at RMIT University Melbourne. The firm's work has been exhibited in Sydney, Melbourne, Glasgow and Tokyo. Important completed projects include Price/O'Reilly House, Redfern, NSW (1995), Davis House, Darlinghurst, NSW (1997), Ruzzene/Leon House, Neutral Bay, NSW (1997), Rose House, Kiama, NSW (2000), Altair Apartments, Kings Cross, NSW (2001), and The Grid Apartments, Rushcutters Bay, NSW (2001). The firm's work has appeared in *10x10*, London: Phaidon (2000); *A+U* (Japan); *Casabella* (Italy); *Monument Magazine* (Australia); *The Architectural Review* (UK); *Architektur und Wohen* (Germany); and *UME* (Australia).

Davis House
photograph © Ross Honeysett

ENGELEN MOORE

A sleek and highly resolved combination of engineering and interior design distinguishes the oeuvre of Engelen Moore. Before becoming an architect, Ian Moore trained and worked as a structural engineering technician in New Zealand. As his father was a builder, Moore had lived in over 34 houses before leaving to work for Ove Arup in London, where he was responsible for detailing offshore oil platforms, and significantly, Norman Foster's Hong Kong and Shanghai Bank. Tina Engelen is the daughter of Dutch émigrés who founded the importing firm of De De Ce (originally the Danish Design Centre) in Sydney. Engelen grew up in an environment where living with the finest industrial and interior design was the norm. As collaborators in an architecture firm, Tina Engelen and Ian Moore's concerns are not for a minimalist style, but in matching the pragmatics of 'space, light and ventilation' with the aesthetics of systems-based interior design.

One of Moore's early projects after graduating in architecture was a six storey prefabricated steel framed apartment building in Port Moresby, New Guinea (1989). This project demonstrated his interests in structure and unit repetition, and it was published under the name of Burley Katon Halliday, the firm where he and Engelen met. As an interior designer, Engelen gained crucial experience there, and realised the importance of 'styling' interiors for marketing purposes. She had also worked as an assistant editor for Herbert Ypma's *Interior Design* magazine, and after leaving Burley Katon Halliday had been briefly in partnership with celebrated furniture designer Mark Newson. It was quite a different pedigree and experience to Moore's engineering and architectural background. His European trip (1990-91) resulted in a passion for the white forms and louvred walls of Spanish architect Jose Coderch, and the belief that on his return, he could create 'simple spaces that dispensed with everything.' Back in Sydney, Moore developed prefabricated bathroom systems, inserting them into the modest house and apartment renovations that characterised his years of sole practice.

The Price/O'Reilly House (1995), in Redfern, brought Engelen and Moore together, and it became the catalyst for public attention and professional success. Located on a rare vacant terrace house site, their clients (one a fashion photographer, the other a hair and make-up artist) wanted a house that doubled as a daylight studio. To satisfy the local council, Engelen Moore produced a 'proportional representation' of two double storey terrace houses, but the house was actually designed and built as a steel portal framed factory. The clients requested white internal walls, and a full height stacking door system was implemented. The furniture could be wheeled away quickly for photo shoots. The entire low-cost and lightweight kit of parts range called 'Easy' was designed by the architects. This house became the prototype for many of Engelen Moore's later house and apartment designs, an Antipodean version of Le Corbusier's Pavilion L'Esprit Nouveau (1925), and it has come to typify the urbane indoor-outdoor room, especially in Sydney.

ENGELEN MOORE

photograph © Ross Honeysett

Rose House. Kiama, NSW. 2000.

In Neutral Bay, the Ruzzene/Leon House (1997), was dictated by another 19th century subdivision shape - a long narrow sliver – with little or no natural light, and minimal ventilation. Engelen Moore adopted the typical gun-barrel corridor plan, but brought in light from a saw-tooth roof and made the free side wall a screen of aluminium louvres that filtered light and air, and lent privacy. Sliding walls diffuse the linearity of the corridor, and the party wall is painted black and acts as a heat sink, radiating warmth in winter.

Similar themes inform Engelen Moore's refurbishment of 19th century buildings in Sydney's inner suburbs. The Davis House, Darlinghurst (1997), is the transformation of a burnt-out three storey Victorian terrace house. All the living spaces of the new town house and lower level apartment have been re-oriented to the rear of the site and its panoramic views. Inside and out, there is a colour coding: everything white is as economical as possible, everything silver is highly detailed and refined. The spiral stair is a dramatic metallic flourish connecting the upper level deck to the roof terrace above the garage. In the Carroll Watson House, Paddington (1998), the palette continues to be minimised and the ecological maxim of 'space, light, ventilation' is repeated with grey linoleum floors, a stair as a thermal chimney, and an outdoor pool which becomes a cooling device to sun-drenched interiors. There is, always, a calculated hierarchy of attention - the house must operate as a breathing machine.

Echoes of the sleek houses of Los Angeles Case Study architects Craig Ellwood and Pierre Koenig can be found, with the same penchant for engineered solutions, industrially produced furniture, and modular divisions. These echoes become even more pronounced with the Rose House, Kiama (2000), two hours south of Sydney - an adaptation of Ellwood's precise linear plans morphed with the visor-like forms of Harry Seidler's 1950s beach houses. The house is a triumph of rural engineering - to resist gale force winds and maximise panoramic views, two vierendeel trusses run the length of the house, sitting on two heavily reinforced concrete block feet (pods). The trusses allow the house to cantilever more than three and a half metres at either end, while the two service cores that pass through the floor assist in bracing the entire structure. With the Louie Chee House (2001) in suburban Drummoyne , the site is defined by a retaining wall which protects a highly modularised steel and glass box, veiled by louvres.

The Altair Apartments, Kings Cross (2001), straddle a four lane traffic tunnel, which dictates an 8.1 metre grid of concrete shear walls, and determines the apartment widths. To the north, a *brise-soleil* sunscreen cantilevers beyond the building's main mass to become a giant billboard for sun-control, while to the east and west, vertical aluminium louvres enable an entirely adjustable face. Altair has been designed to have no air-conditioning, and the kitchen and bathrooms have been planned as freestanding pods within the apartments to allow ventilation across the width of the sixteen level slab. The Grid in Rushcutters Bay (2001), a smaller development of 38 apartments, follows similar principles of cross ventilation, formal modulation based on deep balconies, and a north-facing 'grid' of stacked row house plans with pavilion-type book-ends. The south side of the building is shielded from traffic noise by a lift core, and two layers of glazed screens enclose light courts and ground-floor pools. The Barcom Avenue development at Rushcutters Bay will combine all these elements: attached row-house type, pavilion plan, and apartment stacking.

Adolf Loos once described himself as the 'mason that studies Latin'. Engelen Moore carry on that tradition. Their ideas on repetition, industrial design, and environmental control coalesce in these apartment buildings, and their uncompromising abstract forms now denote major urban landmarks.

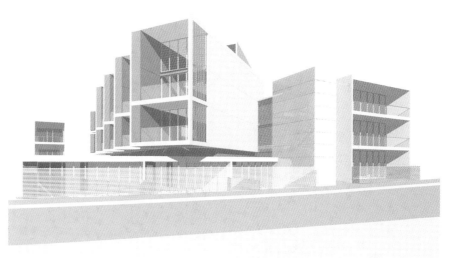

Barcom Avenue Apartments. Rushcutters Bay, NSW. 2001-.

PRICE O'REILLY HOUSE

living room

photograph © Ross Honeysett

ground floor plan

1st floor plan

PRICE O'REILLY HOUSE | Redfern | NSW | **1995**

ENGELEN MOORE

east elevation

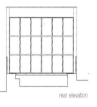

front elevation

rear elevation

cross section

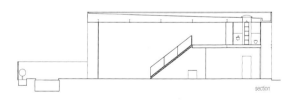

section

west elevation

PRICE O'REILLY HOUSE | Redfern | NSW | **1995**

DAVIS HOUSE

ENGELEN MOORE

photograph © Ross Honeysett

east facade

section

DAVIS HOUSE | Darlinghurst | NSW | **1997**

RUZZENE LEON HOUSE

north elevation

south elevation

section

section

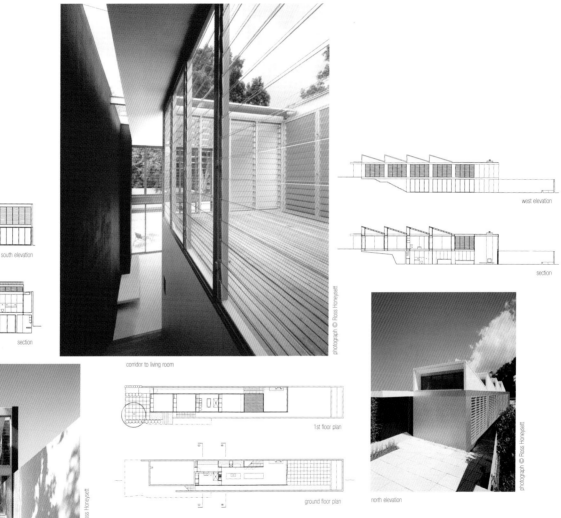

corridor to living room

west elevation

section

1st floor plan

ground floor plan

photograph © Ross Honeysett

south elevation

photograph © Ross Honeysett

north elevation

photograph © Ross Honeysett

ROSE HOUSE

ENGELEN MOORE

photograph © Ross Honeysett

north elevation

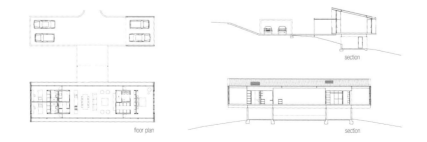

floor plan

section

section

ROSE HOUSE | Kiama | NSW | **2000**

photograph © Ross Honeysett

living room from west

photograph © Ross Honeysett

ROSE HOUSE │ Kiama │ NSW │ **2000**

NEW DIRECTIONS IN AUSTRALIAN ARCHITECTURE

ALTAIR APARTMENTS

north and west elevations

ALTAIR APARTMENTS | Kings Cross | NSW | **2001**

west and south elevations

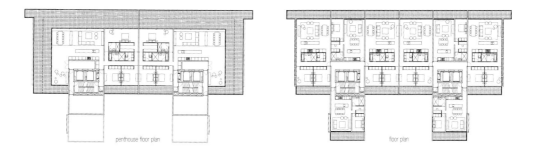

penthouse floor plan

floor plan

ALTAIR APARTMENTS | Kings Cross | NSW | **2001**

CARROLL WATSON HOUSE

ENGELEN MOORE

photograph © Ross Honeysett

ground floor

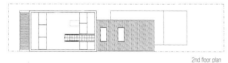

2nd floor plan

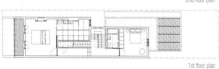

1st floor plan

ground floor plan

photograph © Ross Honeysett

ground floor

CARROLL WATSON HOUSE | Paddington | NSW | **1998**

LOUIE CHEE HOUSE

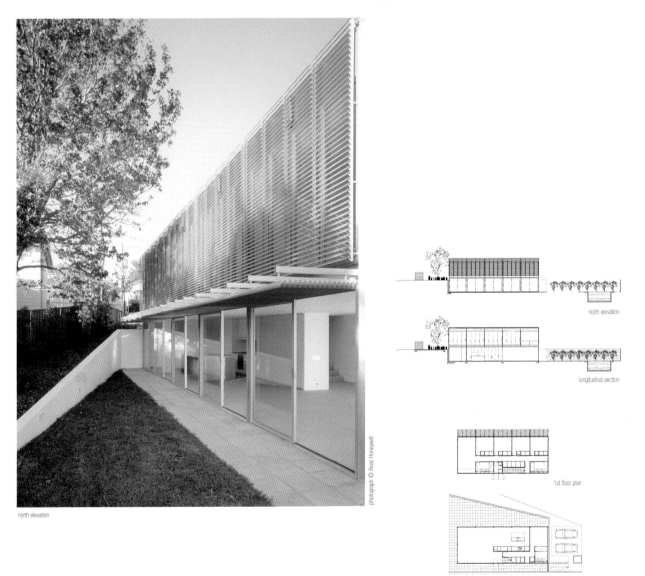

photograph © Ross Honeysett

north elevation

north elevation

longitudinal section

1st floor plan

ground floor plan

THE GRID
APARTMENTS

ENGELEN MOORE

penthouse floor plan

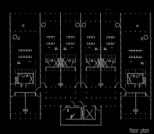

floor plan

THE GRID APARTMENTS | Rushcutters Bay | NSW | 2001

SEAN GODSELL

Sean Godsell (born Melbourne, 1960) graduated in architecture from The University of Melbourne in 1984. After travelling in Japan and Europe in 1985, he worked in London for Sir Denys Lasdun from 1986 to 1988. From 1989-92, Godsell worked for Hassell Architects, Melbourne and in 1994, he formed Godsell Associates Pty Ltd Architects. He has taught design at The University of Melbourne and at RMIT University. In 1999, he completed his Masters of Architecture at RMIT University. The firm's work has been exhibited in Sydney, New York, Copenhagen, Paris and London. Important completed projects include MacSween House, Kensington, Victoria (1995), Godsell House, Kew, Victoria (1998), Woodleigh School Art Faculty, Baxter, Victoria (1999), Carter Tucker House, Breamlea, Victoria (2000), and Future Shack prototype, Kensington, Victoria (2001). Godsell's buildings have appeared in numerous books and journals including *B* (Denmark), *Architectural Record* (USA), *Domus* (Italy), *A+U* (Japan), *DBZ* (Germany) and *The Architectural Review* (UK).

Godsell House

SEAN GODSELL

The architecture of Sean Godsell is informed by craft and the consistent exploration of formal and spatial types. His buildings indicate a wish for 'making architecture well', a difficult task in Australia where, as in most post-industrial nations, craft-skills have dramatically diminished in recent decades. His is an intense practice, formed by observing his architect-father David Godsell (1930-86), whose passion for architecture involved perfection, precision, and a belief in Louis Sullivan's notion of architecture being accomplice to "an unfolding democracy". Acutely aware of Australia's geographic proximity to Asia, Godsell has long been interested in the synergies possible in the contemporary architectures of East and West. A professed admirer of Japanese architect Kazuo Shinohara's scientific rigour in planning and formal refinement, Godsell is fascinated by corridors and their potential as passages, living-galleries, and as tantalising routes to the unfolding of the interior. He talks of 'the connected plan', an interior that can be divided, traversed, or opened up at will.

The first Godsell house, Carlton, Victoria (1993), and the Gandolfo House, Camberwell, Victoria (1994), were early experiments. The former, a three level townhouse on a tight inner city site, was a vertical extrusion where the passage was planned to make the house seem larger than it actually was. The latter was an open-planned linear house on a suburban site, its flat roof supported off a Neutra-like composition of flat roof, steel posts and oversailing beams. In the MacSween House, Kensington, Victoria (1995), Godsell brought the two house types together. Facing the street, the two-bedroom house resembles a modern Ise Shrine, a dwelling as temple to construction. With an extremely small budget, the rationale was to erect the trussed gable roof first and then fit out the building underneath. A constructive logic and a systems approach are evident, lessons learnt from Godsell's experience in Denys Lasdun's London office (1986-88), and his design for the Northern Metropolitan TAFE, Heidelberg, Victoria when working for Hassell Architects (1989-92).

MacSween House. Kensington, Vic. 1995.

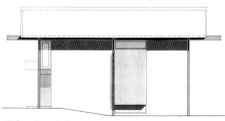

MacSween House elevation

Further experimentation with the 'divided' plan and the building skin can be seen in Godsell's second house for his family (1998), on a steeply sloping site close to the Yarra River in suburban Kew. The rectangular plan is divided down its length by a thickened wall, and sliding screens close down or open up this interior. There is no passage as such. It is an enfilade plan, yet the entire space could be seen as one large passage with a changing width that can be cut off at various points to create isolated rooms. Godsell is interested in the fluid nature of the traditional Japanese house verandah, and the ambiguous nature of space as it is defined, closed, and opened by the *shoji* screen. The Godsell House is veiled on three sides with weathered steel gridded screens, that can be raised or lowered for shade or complete transparency. The rusted steel is rich in colour and texture. When pictured against a garden of grass tussocks and giant boulders, the house appears as a *shibui* war chest, its latch a gridded canopy that flips up to reveal the glass front door. Godsell is adamant that this house is 'not modern'. It is not a restatement of Mies van der Rohe's Farnsworth House (1950), but a counterpoint in texture, structural and spatial concerns. The kitchen table is for living at, not looking at. The house cantilevers 5.5 metres out from its site, though not intended as a deliberate structural feat in the manner of Peter and Dione McIntyre's nearby A-frame house (1955). Due to the economic constraints of building higher, there was no option but to go out and over the street. At the same time, the house does not float but beds itself into the site.

At the Woodleigh School Art Faculty, Baxter, Victoria (1999), Godsell reveals his skills in timber construction. The building is an addition to a celebrated example of 1970s educational architecture by

the Melbourne firm, Jackson Walker. Godsell refers to the diagonal boarding and the structural rhythm of the existing building. His addition is modest. It is an elegant shed with a robust interior of concrete, plaster and raw timber, all predicated on repetition and the discipline of the module. There is about Godsell's work a determinedly aestheticized 'low-tech' position - specific to constricted budgets - that attempts to draw its essence from each commission. Monumental aspiration is achieved through reduced means - rather like the strict ascetic principles of Zen Buddhism, or the purified essentialist position of the Shakers.

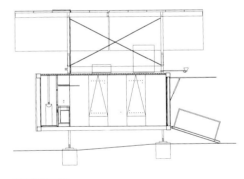

Future Shack section

The adoption of humble technologies lies behind Future Shack (2001), Godsell's self-funded prototype for temporary relief accommodation for homeless people in disaster-struck regions. The universal module of a shipping container, in weathered steel, has been fitted out with an insulated marine plywood interior. Above, a parasol roof acts as an outdoor sleeping platform and thermal barrier, and as a potential support for solar collectors. An echo of the low-cost MacSween house, this roof can be dismantled and packed

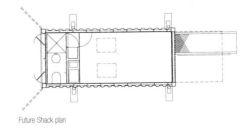

Future Shack plan

away into the container. The legs telescope down to accommodate locations on uneven terrain, and a tow-bar ball on a flat plate pad forms a foot to each leg. Inside, there is a 15 square metre room with two beds that fold into the walls, a skylit kitchen with a fold-down table, and a bathroom. Future Shack is Godsell's answer to the technological visions of Buckminster Fuller, Jean Prouvé and Future Systems - a house for everyman.

The Carter Tucker House (2000), at Breamlea on Victoria's west coast, is a three level timber battened box. Like the Godsell House, Kew, it is edged into the slope. Its view is of wetlands, and the ocean is behind a dune and out of sight. The approach to the house is carefully orchestrated: one walks deep into the site, up the slope beside the apparently mute prism, and enters through a weathered steel portal at mid-level onto a bridge of gridded steel. The rear of the house is a light and airy circulation volume, with a solid wall base finished in hand-striated cement render, like hand-drawn grooves on a finely thrown pot. The top level is an open living/dining/kitchen room recalling Kenzo Tange's Tokyo home (1954), - with timber floors, sliding glass doors and screens. Here, however, ropes do not roll up bamboo blinds, they lift battened shutters. Suddenly, the exterior form of the house comes alive. As the flaps open, the purity of the form is signed as habitation. It is now an adjustable living container, changing its form according to the sun and the wind. The monumental has become the practical.

Future Shack. 2001.

Future Shack interior

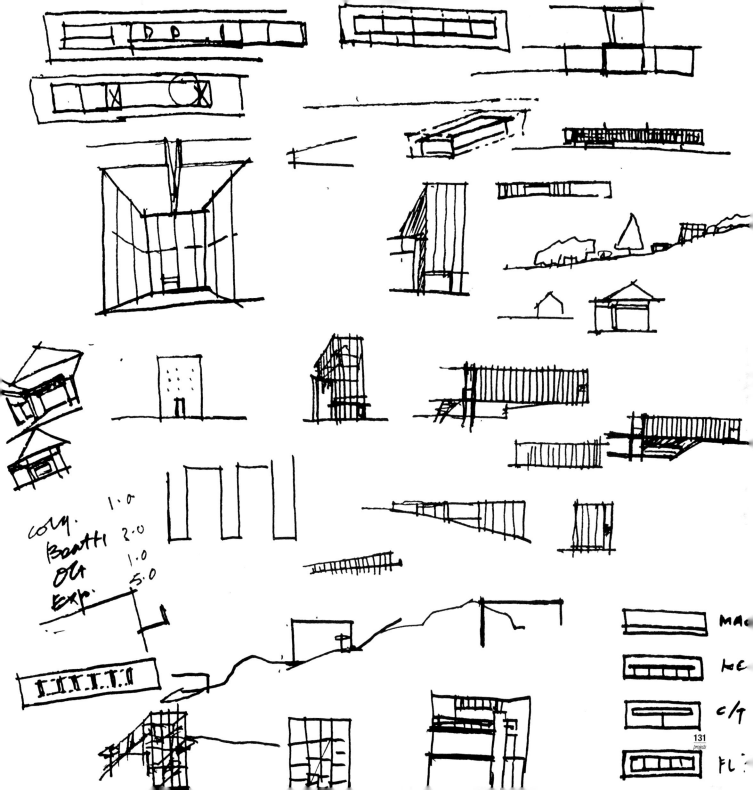

Corg. 1.0
Beatti 2.0
OCA 1.0
Exp 5.0

MA
kC
C/q
FL

NEW DIRECTIONS IN AUSTRALIAN ARCHITECTURE

GODSELL HOUSE

north elevation

GODSELL HOUSE | Kew | Victoria | **1998**

living room

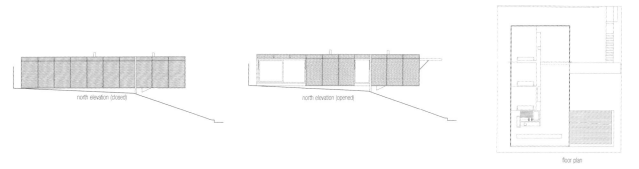

north elevation (closed)

north elevation (opened)

floor plan

CARTER TUCKER HOUSE

SEAN GODSELL

north elevation

SEAN GODSELL

1st floor living room

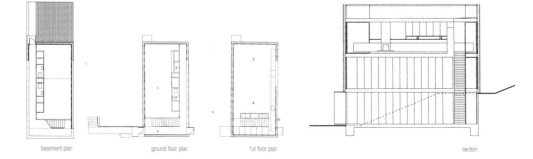

basement plan   ground floor plan   1st floor plan   section

CARTER TUCKER HOUSE | Breamlea | Victoria | 2000

1st floor living room

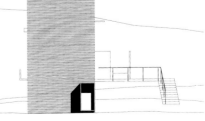

west elevation

north elevation

CARTER TUCKER HOUSE | Breamlea | Victoria | **2000**

WOODLEIGH SCHOOL ART FACULTY

SEAN GODSELL

view from south east

south elevation

section

west elevation

site plan

plan

WOODLEIGH SCHOOL ART FACULTY | Baxter | Victoria | **1999**

JONES COULTER YOUNG

Jones Coulter Young (JCY) was established in 1995. Paul Jones (born Perth WA, 1955), Richard Young (born Sydney, NSW, 1953) and Ross Coulter (born Perth WA, 1956-2000) were the original directors. Elisabetta Guj (born Rome, Italy, 1963) and Andrew Rogerson (born Fremantle WA, 1961) were made directors in 2001. Previously, the original directors had been key founders of Philip Cox Etherington Coulter and Jones (PCECJ) (1986-95). Jones graduated in architecture from the Western Australia Institute of Technology in 1977 and from the Architectural Association in London in 1981. From 1981-85, he worked for Foster Associates in London on Stansted Airport and Renault Headquarters before returning to Perth to form Odden Coulter Etherington and Jones (OCEJ) (1985-86). Coulter graduated with an Honours Degree in Architecture from the Western Australia Institute of Technology in 1979 and remained with JCY until 1998. Young graduated from the Western Australian Institute of Technology in 1975 and formed Hamlin Young Architects prior to joining PCECJ. Guj received an Honours Degree in Architecture at The University of Western Australia in 1985 and joined PCECJ in 1988. Rogerson graduated from the Western Australian Institute of Technology in 1984 and joined OCEJ in 1986. Important JCY completed projects include the West Australian Newspaper Headquarters, Herdsman, WA (1997); Learmonth International Airport, Exmouth, WA (1999); Ansett Customer Contact Centre, Joondalup, WA (2000); and the Science and Health Building, Edith Cowan University, Joondalup Campus, WA (2001).

Learmonth International Airport

JONES COULTER YOUNG

In Perth, architectural specialisations grow and recede as the city's economic cycles rise and fall. Expertise in highly specific building types is developed rapidly by multi-disciplinary practices. When Jones Coulter Young (JCY) was formed in 1995, the Perth suburbs were expanding to the north and south at an astounding rate. The city was upgrading its freeways and its public transport infrastructure, and a boom in university building was underway.

At Subiaco, the new railway station and public square (1995), articulated JCY's expertise in high-tech structures and urban design. The white steel butterfly-roof canopies signalled a double pedigree. Firstly, JCY director Paul Jones had worked for Foster Associates on similar infrastructure and institutional projects, and fellow JCY directors shared his interests in building detailed resolutions of program. Secondly, JCY had emerged in 1995 from the previous partnership (1986-1995), of Philip Cox Etherington Coulter and Jones (PCECJ) of which Paul Jones, Richard Young and Ross Coulter were directors, and Elisabetta Guj and Andrew Rogerson were associate directors. PCECJ projects such as Joondalup Railway Station (1992), and the Advanced Manufacturing Technologies Centre, East Perth, WA (1992, and its later additions (1995) by JCY), involved the JCY directors and employed a vocabulary of white painted steel masts, attached sunshade baffles, and sophisticated skin technology. PCECJ had also designed the New Technologies Building at Curtin University of Technology, Bentley, WA (1994), a project which emerged from a design process involving Paul Jones and Elisabetta Guj. This building - a surprising contrast to the East Perth and Joondalup buildings - is faced in polychromatic striped brickwork and studded with huge geometric cutouts. It is the subsequent fusion of highly resolved systems design with boldly sculptural and colourful formal expression that has characterised JCY's work over the past six years.

The West Australian Newspapers Building, Herdsman, WA (1996), is typical of JCY's closely examined programmatic responses. The team-based working environment for 750 people is housed in two parallel office wings, separated by a large entry atrium. The sun is kept at bay, and the atrium acts as a mediator between external heat and controlled internal temperatures. The same assiduous adherence to function is explored in a relatively new building type, the 'call-centre', at the Ansett Customer Contact Centre, Joondalup, WA (2000). The two wings are separated by a staff garden, and the call-centre wing of uninterrupted floor space is enlivened by a brightly coloured undulating ceiling.

Ansett Customer Contact Centre. Joondalup, WA. 2000.

Old Tannery. Fremantle, WA. 1999.

Old Tannery

Innovative program response also lies behind the reconfiguration of the boarding houses at St. Hilda's (2001), an Anglican girls' school in the suburb of Mosman Park. Responsible for the masterplan and new infill work, JCY expanded corridors and orchestrated picturesque routes of colour between intimate gathering spaces. The architectural vocabulary deferred to the brick colours and pitched roof forms of the existing 1970s buildings, but reinterpreted their textures with red and pink precast concrete panels randomly sandblasted or left smooth. The Old Tannery project (1999), situated in the heart of Fremantle, comprises a small cluster of offices and a residence integrated within the fabric of the 1920s WA Tanners & Fellmongers factory. The sophisticated open plan design of the residence and offices contrasts with the fabric of the original factory, creating a rich living and working environment.

With the Learmonth International Airport (1999), 30km south of Exmouth on the North West Cape, JCY's blend of systems design and vigorous formal expression has created an unforgettable landmark. Conceived as a key link in the tourism development of WA's Gascoyne Region, the airport makes reference to the forms and colours of the nearby Ningaloo Reef, and is an astonishing and exotic object in the harsh red sand landscape. JCY's furniture designs also make reference to the nearby reef, and resemble starfish, nudibranches, and sea urchins. Despite this excitable *architecture parlante*, the airport building has a decidely rational aspect: its major spine comprises tilt-slab concrete walls; the amoebic parasols and the anodised aluminium fins shade the interior from sun; and all the steel members were prefabricated to expedite construction at a remote location. The building has a totemic quality, and like any emblazoned indigenous implement, the aim is twofold: an efficient new airport, and an instantly memorable gateway.

Similar distinctive architectural flourishes, matched with state of the art systems-based facilities, characterise the Science and Health Building at Edith Cowan University's Joondalup Campus, WA (2001). From the outset, the brief had two major requirements: a signature building for an emerging 'young' university, and ecological sustainability. To the north and south, the building's face is louvred to keep the sun out of all laboratories, class and tutorial rooms. In the courtyard between the two deep linear blocks is a blue cylindrical lift core. To the west, facing the central lake of the main campus, the building is highly expressive. Giant curving concrete forms bulge outward like expanding armadillo shells, while a deep eave floats above. It is as if the concrete has been given full plasticity. A tapering elliptical form contains two lecture theatres, and circulation links have been reinforced by JCY's invitation to artist

Andrew Leslie to add three components to the building's design. The first, a line of colourful graduated posts, marches through the landscape and signs the main entry, where JCY's suspended concrete wall is punched with diatom shapes. The second component is the collection of coloured metal panels attached to the west-sited 'bio-mechanics box', and the third component is the series of columns painted by Leslie in the void of the main entry lobby, where JCY have added enigmatic urn-like columns supporting stairs - the final curious specimens in a building dedicated to biological research.

JCY's projects for the City of Stirling Civic Centre, Stirling, WA (2001-), and the Curtin Business School and School of Physiotherapy, Curtin University of Technology, Bentley, WA (2001-), continue these design themes. The former is a series of civic offices and council chambers with a brief for civic presence and energy efficiency. The latter is another gateway building, complete with a stainless steel sheathing of the campus water tower. In Perth, it would be very easy to let climate dictate every formal component of a building's design. In JCY's case, responsibility to climate is taken for granted. There is much more to their architecture - responsibility does not negate sheer formal joy. There is a functional necessity to artifice - art and science need not be exclusive, but mutually supporting aims.

St Hilda's Anglican Girls School. Mosman Park, WA. 2001.

NEW DIRECTIONS IN AUSTRALIAN ARCHITECTURE

LEARMONTH INTERNATIONAL AIRPORT

west facade

west facade

LEARMONTH INTERNATIONAL AIRPORT | Exmouth | WA | **1999**

west elevation

JONES COULTER YOUNG

LEARMONTH INTERNATIONAL AIRPORT | Exmouth | WA | **1999**

east elevation

cafe and departure lounge

floor plan

north elevation

south elevation

LEARMONTH INTERNATIONAL AIRPORT | Exmouth | WA | **1999**

NEW DIRECTIONS IN AUSTRALIAN ARCHITECTURE

SCIENCE & HEALTH BUILDING
EDITH COWAN UNIVERSITY

lift core from courtyard

SCIENCE & HEALTH BUILDING | Edith Cowan University | Joondalup | WA | 2001

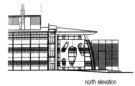

north elevation

1st floor plan

ground floor foyer

SCIENCE & HEALTH BUILDING | Edith Cowan University | Joondalup | WA | 2001

JONES COULTER YOU

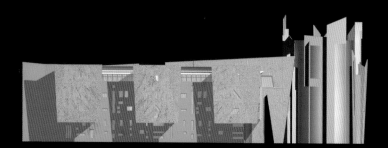

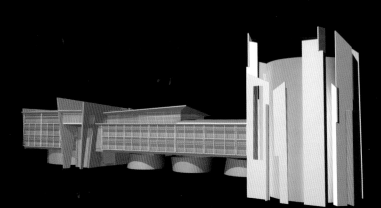

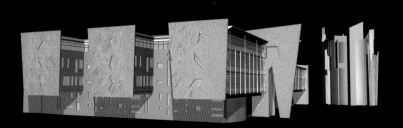

CITY OF STIRLING CIVIC BUILDING

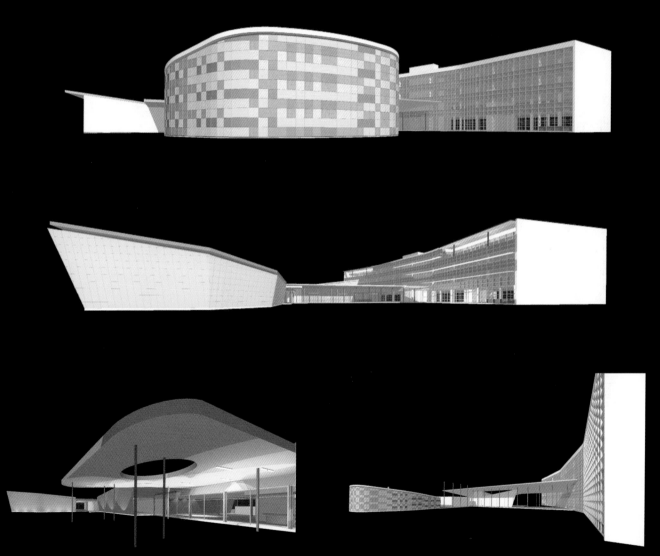

LYONS ARCHITECTS

Corbett Lyon (born Melbourne, 1955) graduated in architecture from The University of Melbourne in 1977 and gained his Masters of Architecture from University of Pennsylvania in 1980. From 1980-81, he worked with Venturi Rauch and Scott Brown in Philadelphia and New York. Cameron Lyon (born Melbourne, 1957) graduated from The University of Melbourne in 1979. Cameron Lyon and Corbett Lyon formed the practice Lyon + Lyon in 1982, which later became Lyon Lyon Hilbert. Cameron Lyon worked as Principal Design Architect for the Victorian State Government from 1996 to 1998. Carey Lyon (born Melbourne, 1959) graduated from The University of Melbourne in 1982 and gained his Masters of Architecture from RMIT University in 1995. He worked for Perrott Lyon Mathieson from 1985 to 1996 and established Lyons in 1996 with Corbett Lyon. Cameron Lyon joined the firm in 1998. Corbett Lyon has taught at The University of Melbourne. Carey Lyon has taught at The University of Melbourne and at RMIT University. The firm's work has been exhibited in Venice, Sydney and Melbourne. Important completed projects by the firm include: Box Hill Institute of TAFE, Nelson Campus Stage 2, Box Hill, Victoria (1999), *City of Fiction*, Australian Pavilion Exhibit, Venice, Italy (2000); Swinburne University (TAFE), Lilydale Lake Campus Stage 2, Lilydale, Victoria (2001, with Perrott Lyon Mathieson); On-line Training Centre, Victoria University of Technology, St. Albans, Victoria (2001); and Sunshine Hospital, St Albans, Victoria (2001). The firm's work has appeared in numerous books and journal articles including: Peter Zellner, *Pacific Edge: Contemporary Architecture on the Pacific Rim*, London: Thames and Hudson (1998); *Architecture Australia*; *Architectural Review Australia*; *Backlogue*; *Bauwelt* (Germany); *Monument*; and *Transition*.

Swinburne University, Stage 2.
Lilydale Lake Campus

LYONS ARCHITECTS

Lyons are fascinated with surface and representation, with images as commodity, and the way in which a 'thin', often expedient, building skin can become a potent bearer of meaning. Most of their buildings, institutional or educational, are to be found on Melbourne's outer suburban periphery. They sit on tough, unforgiving sites, where aesthetic gestures on a super-graphic scale are the only creators of a recognisable, let alone definable, context.

The firm of Lyons, established in 1996 is run by three brothers, Corbett, Cameron, and Carey Lyon, who come from a long, almost dynastic, architectural line in Melbourne. It is thus quite unexpected that this firm appears utterly unconventional in its approach to making architecture. It is as if their thinking could have been determined by reacting against their own history, yet precedents exist in their lineage for this non-conformity. Their grandfather Leslie M Perrott was an early 20th century advocate of the concrete house, as well as a pioneering promoter of social housing. Now Lyons are preoccupied with that most contemporary of cultural conditions - the acknowledgement that the forms and conventions of seeing, making, and using architecture have shifted ground dramatically over the last two decades.

Early signs of an alternative approach to making form are evident in two important projects completed before the formation of Lyons. Carey Lyon, when working with Perrott Lyon Mathieson, designed Building B, Swinburne University (TAFE), Lilydale Lake, Victoria (1996-98), and the first stage of the Goulburn Ovens Institute of TAFE, Benalla, Victoria (1996-98). The former is a giant and folded landscape sign, a remnant slice of quarried escarpment risen from below, depicted as polychromatic brick pixels on one side and rolling green hills on the other. It is a building that suggests an uncertain reciprocity between landscape and object. At Benalla, a cruciform steel shed has its faces and its form striated like landscape contours, coloured and undulating.

Lyons' most critically demonstrative work, the City of Fiction installation, was exhibited in Sydney in 1999, and then at the Venice Biennale in 2000. This work encapsulated their thinking about the contemporary city. The installation took the form of a massive wall of brick-sized postcards stacked in stretcher bond. As a total image, it depicted a skyline view of Melbourne taken at 5am from a taxi speeding over the Bolte Bridge enroute to the airport. The image, in its pixilated 'brickwork' form showed a generic skyscraper city. From behind the highest tower, there emerged a sunburst. Was this Enlightenment? Or a clever play on Lyonel Feininger's famous woodblock of the sunburst behind the cathedral of socialism that symbolised the birth of the Bauhaus? At a closer scale, each postcard showed a work by Lyons or a pithy aphorism about the nature of their practice: "Scratching the Surface"; "Surface not form"; "From authenticity to real fiction"; "EYE deology", and so on.

Paper thin and ornamental - these then are the provocative possibilities and also the potentials for experiment in Lyons' work. In all of their building, the early ideas of Robert Venturi find an echo, along with his recent musings on iconography and electronics. Flattened images - intellectually rich and digitally reproduced - adorn robust and pragmatic sheds with strong internal volumetric gestures. With the Stage 2 extension to the Box Hill Institute of TAFE's Nelson Campus, Box Hill, Victoria (1999), Lyons graphically indicate the 4 metre width of a corridor on the external wall. They then trace its path up the wall and across the roof. The internal result is a white curving public street, a domical shingled volume, and a curving luminescent skylight. The dome (which contains a lecture theatre) and an upper gallery are clad in fibreboard shingles, and painted in the colours of pixellated satellite pictures of the earth.

Similar ideas appear in the other Lyons buildings designed for Box Hill Institute of TAFE. At the Centre for Automotive Studies, Elgar Campus (2000), the west-facing wall is like a giant tyre tread created from a luminous wall of striated corrugated fibreglass. Internally, cranked steel portals and skylight strips create an expressionistic space of production. At the Whitehorse Campus, a golden computer generated image of a fragment of Hans Scharoun's National Library is held above an existing building, as the facing to a new infill project (2001).

At the Lilydale Lake campus for Swinburne University (TAFE) Stage 2, Lyons added to the earlier first stage building with an addition (2001) that was a virtual black and white 'xerox' of the original. Where they cut the building off, Lyons hatched it as one might do to a drawing to indicate the bluntness of the cut. On the south, sprays of white brickwork upon the most mundane of brick shells add a curious magnified image. The same technique of scaling the skin is deployed at the Victoria University of Technology (VUT) Plumbing School, Sunshine, Victoria (2000), an addition conceived as a 'background' to an existing adjacent 'billboard' building. The east façade thus became a transparent Tintoretto sky full of floating clouds. The building skin is comprised of blue metal panels with white acrylic "clouds".

Marine and Freshwater Resources Institute. Queenscliff, Victoria. 2001-.

With each project, Lyons determine the image to be explored from the immediate context or directly from their client's brief. At the On-line Training Centre, VUT St. Albans Campus, Victoria (2001), the metal 'Vitrapanel' cladding system could have any digital image imprinted upon it, and Lyons chose a psychedelic composition of melted yellow and brown. From afar it appears as if it is the camouflaging pelt of a jungle animal, and seen above a surreal landscape of bare rocks, this skin is gorgeous and strange. The inflecting and looming forms of the new Sunshine Hospital at St.

Albans, Victoria (2001), inspire similar feelings of disbelief. From the Western Ring Road, the long slab of the hospital appears as if rendered at speed. It is a giant billboard. Lyons describe the vibrant yellow, orange and mauve bricks decorating the south façade as a 'kind of permanent sunshine with a regular array of bay windows marking individual rooms along the stretched skin wall.' This scheme has a deliberately painterly aspect, an impressionistic interest in faux depth and colour.

Lyons' preoccupation with skins does not limit their experiments in form-making. Their project for the Marine and Freshwater Resources Institute, located on The Narrows, a sensitive coastal area at Queenscliff, Victoria (2001-), is a 'green building' with the landscape literally wrapping up and over the roof. Landscape becomes a cultural object - the building is a crease in the dunes. At RMIT University's city campus, the unbuilt project for a Sports and Education Facility is an insertion of a huge pliable tube, which dog-legs around an existing 19th century hotel. The ends of the tube are glazed, highly 'polished' cut ends, revealing the functions within, like the workings of a giant co-axial cable. Its casing constantly shifts texture and transparency according to the cranking of the structure and the passage of the sun.

While the aesthetic of the skin is critical, there is a frank acceptance of the limits of contemporary construction practice and material longevity. Many of these Lyons buildings have been built on extremely modest budgets, but they are large, and they respond to the scale of the urban periphery in a way which no other practice in Australia is prepared to do. They compete and co-habit with mega-marts and malls, with the dimensions of the highway and the intersection, and with the horizon and the sky. In short, these buildings suggest a New World urban scenography.

Images from 'City of Fiction' installation

GOULBURN OVENS INSTITUTE OF TAFE

LYONS ARCHITECTS

BUILDING B SWINBURNE UNIVERSITY LILYDALE LAKE CAMPUS

BUILDING B, SWINBURNE UNIVERSITY (TAFE) | Lilydale Lake Campus | Lilydale | Victoria | **1996-98**
as Perrott Lyon Mathieson

BOX HILL INSTITUTE OF TAFE
NELSON CAMPUS

LYONS ARCHITECTS

SUNSHINE HOSPITAL

NEW DIRECTIONS IN AUSTRALIAN ARCHITECTURE

CENTRE FOR AUTOMOTIVE STUDIES
BOX HILL INSTITUTE OF TAFE

STAGE 2 SWINBURNE UNIVERSITY LILYDALE LAKE CAMPUS

LYONS ARCHITECTS

STAGE 2, SWINBURNE UNIVERSITY (TAFE) | Lilydale Lake Campus | Lilydale | Victoria | **2001**
in association with Perrott Lyon Mathieson

VICTORIA UNIVERSITY OF TECHNOLOGY PLUMBING SCHOOL

SPORTS AND EDUCATION FACILITY
RMIT UNIVERSITY

LYONS ARCHITECTS

image courtesy of Lyons Architects

SPORTS AND EDUCATION FACILITY, RMIT UNIVERSITY | Melbourne | Victoria | (unbuilt)

VICTORIA UNIVERSITY OF TECHNOLOGY ON-LINE TRAINING CENTRE

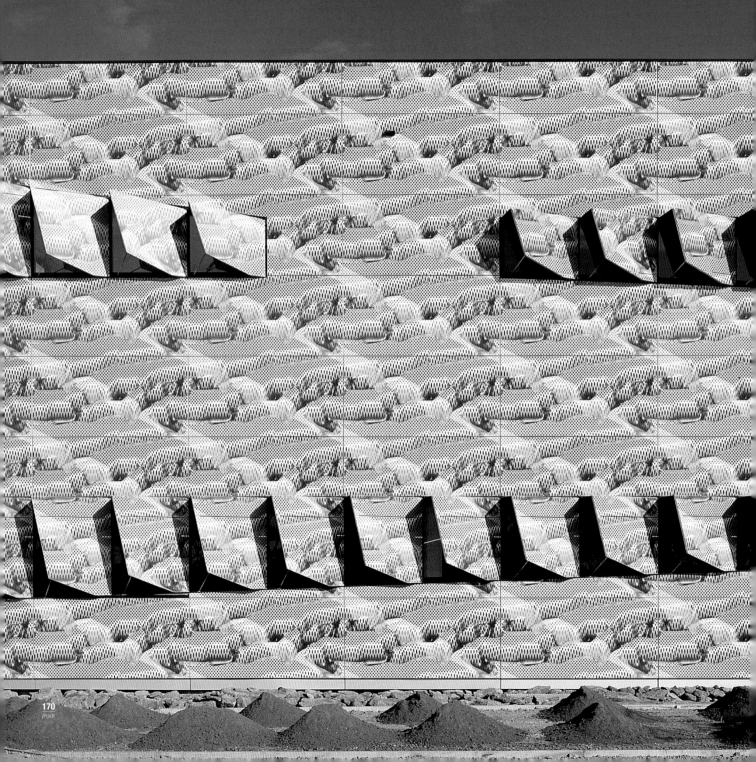

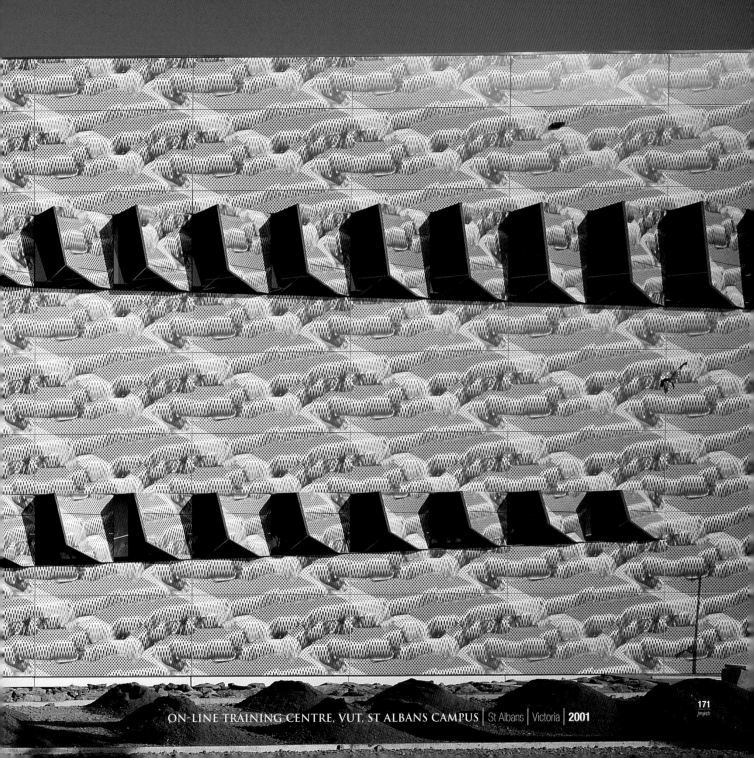

ON-LINE TRAINING CENTRE, VUT, ST ALBANS CAMPUS | St Albans | Victoria | 2001

NATION FENDER
KATSALIDIS

Bob Nation (born Melbourne, 1943) graduated from Hobart Technical College in 1970 and gained his Masters of Architecture from the University of Toronto in 1972. On his return to Hobart, he founded the firm of Heffernan Nation Rees and Viney which became Heffernan Nation Viney in 1979. Nation moved to Hong Kong in 1981 as design director of Yuncken Freeman HK. He then worked under his own name on projects in Hong Kong, Malaysia, China, Indonesia, Scotland and Spain. He has taught at the University of Hong Kong, University of Melbourne, RMIT, and Tasmanian College of Advanced Education. Karl Fender (born Haarlem, The Netherlands 1947) graduated from RMIT in 1975 and gained his Masters of Architecture from Harvard University in 1979. As a student he worked for Romberg & Boyd (1968-72) and after graduation, worked in London for Farrell Grimshaw (1975-76) and in Rome for Brown Daltas & Associates (1976-79). From 1980 to 1985, he was a director of Gunn Williams Fender. From 1985 to 1988, he worked in Hong Kong for CRS-Sirrine, then Wong Tung & Partners. In 1988, he became a director of Axia in Melbourne. In 1990, he and Nation established Nation Fender Pty Ltd. Nonda Katsalidis (born Athens, Greece, 1951) graduated from the University of Melbourne in 1976 and gained his Masters of Architecture from RMIT University in 1992. From 1979 to 1983, he was in sole practice before forming Katsalidis & Partners in 1984. In 1988, his firm amalgamated with Greenhatch & Partners to form Axia. In 1990, Katsalidis left Axia to re-establish Katsalidis Pty Ltd. Nation Fender Katsalidis (NFK) was established in 1996. Important completed works by NFK include the Ian Potter Museum of Art, University of Melbourne, Victoria (1999); Republic Tower, Melbourne, Victoria (2000); and the Sidney Myer Asia Centre, University of Melbourne, Victoria (2001).

Melbourne Terraces (sculpture by Peter Corlett)

NATION FENDER KATSALIDIS

When the Melbourne-based firm of Nation Fender Katsalidis (NFK) was established in 1996, its three principal directors brought together a wealth of design skill and experience. In previous partnerships since the 1970s, all had designed and built major commercial and residential commissions. Bob Nation and Karl Fender had both worked in Hong Kong during the 1980s and had collaborated on Muang Thong Thani, Bangkok, Thailand (1990-95), the complete urban design and construction of a new city with a population of 500,000 people. Adopting a rationalist Late Modern vocabulary, the distinctive visual characteristic of this development was the formal modelling that provided coherence to such a massive undertaking. Nonda Katsalidis had worked mainly in Melbourne on numerous residential and commercial commissions. These projects were all highly sculpted with an intense interest in materials, their textures, and their capacity to weather. The Katsalidis buildings are landmarks demonstrating the powerful urban impact of vigorous formalism.

In 1991, Katsalidis with Axia (a firm which Katsalidis had co-founded in 1988 but left in 1990) completed 171 La Trobe Street, Melbourne and the Argus Centre, Melbourne. Both high rise towers were exuberant collages of elements that recalled Constructivist experiments in dynamic composition. At the Argus Centre, layers of facades and the implied intersection of three dimensional forms break down the building's scale. The podium and foyer are veneered in all manner of marble, and with an inverted and truncated cone provide a theatrical street level setting. In both towers, the virtuosity of the composition transcends empty corporate formalism and challenged conventional ideas of how a tower might look in the Australian city.

At the domestic scale, Katsalidis also questioned traditional formal preconceptions. A beach house designed for his own family at St Andrews Beach (1992), on the Mornington Peninsula south of Melbourne, resembles a washed-up cargo crate - a weathered box built to withstand the elements. The simple linear plan has a raised volume over the living spaces clad with rusted steel. A lowered section contains the bedrooms. The skeleton of the house is a hefty hardwood frame left to weather, infilled with stacked horizontal timber slabs. On the wild Victorian coast, this house has been built to buffet the wind and the sand.

Katsalidis' interests cannot be dismissed as indulgent formalism. After the 1987 stockmarket crash in Australia, architectural attention was drawn to issues of urban consolidation. Melbourne City Council instituted 'Postcode 3000', a scheme that encouraged the refurbishment of existing buildings for housing, and the building of new inner city apartments. In 1994, Katsalidis set new standards for apartment design in the Australian city. His Melbourne Terrace Apartments were the central city's answer to the

Spring Street Apartments. Melbourne, Vic. 1999.

Roman *palazzine* of the 1950s, the speculative apartments that explored the exuberant decorative and formal potential available to an urban façade. Sixty-five apartments were housed over six floors in single level, mezzanine, and two-storey penthouse combinations. Katsalidis enriched his facades with copper oxide-etched balcony slabs, weathered metal, mannered window surrounds, glass blocks, serrated edges to brutish off-form concrete, and a roofline that invites a description such as "post-Apocalyptic Baroque". Other similarly bold apartment building designs followed, including the St Leonards residential development in the beachside suburb of St. Kilda (1996), which rejuvenated the idea of the walk-up apartment block with a rational parti of four stairwells, each serving six apartments. The exterior overlay has vigorous individuality and material richness, and the penthouse level roofline varies between each stairwell. Unifying elements were the liver-brick front wall and the flaring glazed roof canopies at entry level. The Silos residential conversion in Richmond (1996), entailed the refurbishment of four existing wheat silos as a residential tower of six three-bedroom apartments (one per floor) with a double storey penthouse. At each level, three of the silos contain bedrooms, while the fourth has a stair and bathroom. A lift tower, service block, and a living room which terminates in an arrowhead-shaped terrace, were added to the north face of the silos. The resulting composition utilizing off-form concrete, rusted steel balustrades, and crown of thorns eaves, is a brutish totem to inner city living.

Several more apartment buildings designed by NFK have been added to Melbourne's skyline since 1996. The key to the success of these designs has been a distinctive exterior enclosing a simple functional shell which can be fitted out to any buyer's wishes. Two central Melbourne developments, the Spring Street Apartments (1999), and the Republic Tower (2000), have confirmed the return of urbane domesticity to the Australian city. The Republic Tower has the height of a corporate office tower, with the sculptural profile of an armour-clad Japanese samurai. Off-form concrete, stainless steel and glass reflect a new refinement to the firm's work. Street level shops with a café or restaurant mean that the 'fit' with the city is maintained. There is also a 'signing' of Melbourne made by the use of rough-cut bluestone on Queen St, with a gutsy timber pergola on La Trobe St. An NFK initiative, the Visible Art Foundation, regularly commissions artists to produce a constantly changing public exhibition on the street corner.

NFK also design for institutional clients. The responses are more measured when a new building or addition must defer to a precinct or a context. At the Bendigo Art Gallery, Bendigo, Victoria (1995-), NFK had to partially remove a 1960s addition, and add to a 19th century arcaded polychromatic brick building. The new red brick addition, with a Scarpa-esque entry arch and protrusions of steel and glass, is a cool contextual re-knitting of old and new. At the University of Melbourne, the Cubist play of forms of the Ian Potter Museum of Art (1999) on Swanston, St is a subdued deferral to the adjacent 1970s tan-brick laboratory and teaching blocks. The building's interlocking planes become the perfect backdrop for Christine O'Loughlin's bas-relief sculpture 'Cultural Rubble', a riot of fragments of classical architecture, vases and urns, and the limbs and heads of Canova figures. Internally, a similar planar palette conforms to the 'white walls' language of the modern art gallery, and provides the setting for a soaring Napier Waller stained-glass window. Further south on Swanston St, NFK's Sidney Myer Asia Centre (2001), adopts the Potter Museum's architectural dialect. NFK have created their own linguistic context. The building sits on V-shaped concrete struts, and at the northern end, a huge rusted steel sculpture - the last work of the late Akio Makigawa - becomes the building's bookend. Above, a black enamelled panel façade has its

World Tower. Sydney, NSW. 2001-.

image courtesy of NFK digital impression by Bizjig

glazed eastern face protected by a series of vertical baffles. Here, NFK advance the formal qualities of Late Modernism as appropriate to the university's public face, a memory of the productive building phase of the 1950s on the campus.

A suggestion of the worldliness of NFK's large scale proposals for the Australian city can be seen in their mixed-use projects, now under construction, for the Eureka Tower, Melbourne, Victoria (2001-), and World Tower, Sydney, NSW (2001-). Both are highly modelled, impossibly tall, and each will become urban landmarks in their respective cities. Their expression refers not to Manhattan, but to New World skyscraper cities where Melbourne and Sydney join Hong Kong, Kuala Lumpur, Singapore and Shanghai in a new urbanism of the totemic and the visually spectacular.

171 LA TROBE STREET

NATION FENDER KATSALIDIS

west elevation

north elevation

171 LA TROBE STREET | Melbourne | Victoria | **1991**
as Axia

ARGUS CENTRE

east elevation

south elevation

ARGUS CENTRE | Melbourne | Victoria | **1991**

as Axia

ST ANDREWS BEACH HOUSE

NATION FENDER KATSALIDIS

section

plan

north elevation

ST ANDREWS BEACH HOUSE | St Andrews | Victoria | **1992**
as Katsalidis Architects

MUANG THONG THANI
INDUSTRIAL BUILDINGS

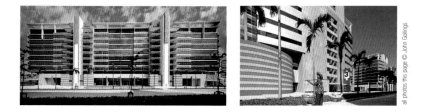

all photos this page © John Gollings

MUANG THONG THANI | Bangkok | Thailand | **1990-95**
as Nation Fender Architects

MELBOURNE TERRACES

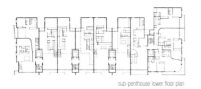

sub-penthouse lower floor plan

east elevation

north elevation

MELBOURNE TERRACES | Melbourne | Victoria | **1994**
as Katsalidis Architects

NATION FENDER KATSALIDIS

ST LEONARDS APARTMENTS

west elevation

west elevation

east elevation

1st floor plan

ST LEONARDS APARTMENTS | St Kilda | Victoria | **1996**
as Katsalidis Architects

SILO APARTMENTS

north facade

SILO APARTMENTS | Richmond | Victoria | **1996**

as Katsalidis Architects

east elevation

levels 2-6 floor plan   level 7 penthouse floor plan   level 8 penthouse floor plan

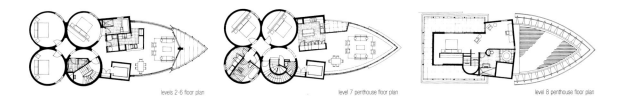

SILO APARTMENTS | Richmond | Victoria | **1996**
as Katsalidis Architects

IAN POTTER MUSEUM OF ART

east facade

IAN POTTER MUSEUM OF ART | University of Melbourne | Victoria | **1999**

as Katsalidis Architects

east elevation

1st floor atrium, featuring the Leckie Window (1935), by Napier Waller

Existing Gallery

Swanston Street

site plan

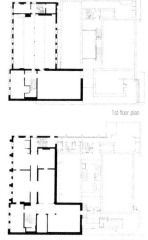

1st floor plan

Ground floor plan

IAN POTTER MUSEUM OF ART | University of Melbourne | Victoria | **1999**
as Katsalidis Architects

REPUBLIC TOWER

east elevation

REPUBLIC TOWER | Melbourne | Victoria | **2000**
as Katsalidis Architects

NATION FENDER KATSALIDIS

north east corner

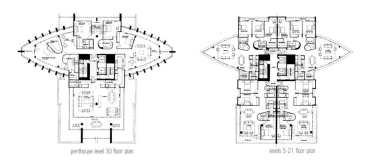

penthouse level 30 floor plan

levels 5-21 floor plan

east elevation

REPUBLIC TOWER | Melbourne | Victoria | **2000**
as Katsalidis Architects

SIDNEY MYER ASIA CENTRE

ground floor plan

1st floor plan

east elevation

north elevation

NATION FENDER KATSALIDIS

BENDIGO ART GALLERY

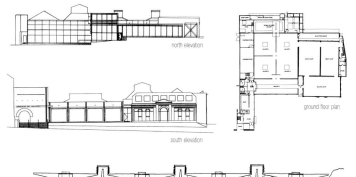

north elevation

south elevation

ground floor plan

section

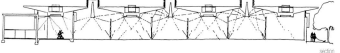

BENDIGO ART GALLERY | Bendigo | Victoria | **1995-**

EUREKA TOWER

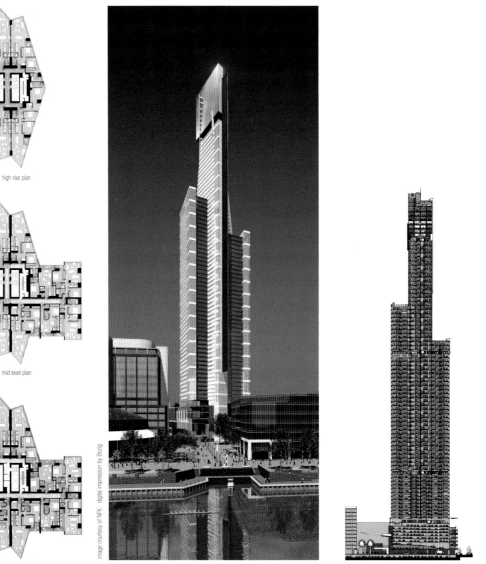

high rise plan

mid level plan

low rise plan

image courtesy of NFK digital impression by Bozig

elevation

NATION FENDER KATSALIDIS

EUREKA TOWER | Melbourne | Victoria | **2001-**

WORLD TOWER

image courtesy of NFK   digital impression by Bizag

high rise plan

mid rise plan

low rise plan

WORLD TOWER | Sydney | NSW | **2001-**

STUTCHBURY AND PAPE

Peter Stutchbury (born Sydney, 1954) graduated in architecture from The University of Newcastle in 1978. Phoebe Pape (born Pietermaritzburg, South Africa, 1959) studied art at the Canberra College of Advanced Education, National School of Art, Canberra, and the Shillito Design School in Sydney before graduating in landscape architecture at Canberra University in 1984. Stutchbury and Pape established a joint practice in 1991. Stutchbury has taught design for more than ten years at The University of Newcastle, and is currently Conjoint Professor. The firm's work has been exhibited in London, Stuttgart, Sydney, Adelaide, and Melbourne. Important completed projects include the Israel House, Paradise Beach, NSW (1986-92); Design Faculty, University of Newcastle, NSW (1994, in conjunction with EJE Architects); Sydney International Archery Park, Homebush Bay, NSW (1998); Clareville House, NSW (1999); Bay House, Watsons Bay, NSW (2001); and the Life Sciences Research Link Building, University of Newcastle, NSW (2001, in association with Suters Architects). The firm's work has been the subject of a monograph: Philip Drew, *Peter Stutchbury: of people and places - between the bush and the beach*, Sydney: Pesaro Publishing (2000), and has appeared in numerous books and journals including *10x10*, London: Phaidon (2000), *B* (Denmark), *Architecture Australia*, *Monument*, and *Architectural Review Australia*.

Bay House

STUTCHBURY AND PAPE

An external dream of Australian architecture has long been the search for Adam's house in Paradise, the desire for renewal through a return to the core of ideals that brought forth the primitive hut. The work of Sydney-based Peter Stutchbury and Phoebe Pape can be regarded as the natural heir to this constructed myth. Their buildings evoke terms like essence, harmony, and repose - concepts that have become increasingly unachievable and impossibly idealist. Yet some myths, born from idealism, do have substance.

Most of the houses designed by Stutchbury and Pape can be found on the neck of land north of Sydney that forms the Barrenjoey Peninsula. To the west lies Pittwater. To the east lies the Pacific Ocean and a stretch of coastline that includes the golden crescents of beaches like Newport, Bilgola, Whale Beach, Palm Beach - and Avalon, named after the 'earthly paradise' of Arthurian legend. The sublime landscape gives this peninsula startling definition. An early Stutchbury house that brought the firm national recognition was the Israel House, Paradise Beach, NSW (1986-92), - a hand-built three level Arthurian tower of the Antipodes, made of timber and topped by a lilting curved roof. The Wedge House, Whale Beach, NSW (2001), perched high above a favoured surfing location of the same name, shares a similarly idyllic site but divides its plan into two triangles - public and private, timber and masonry. Atop a slatted timber wall and covered by a simple yet dynamic mono-slope roof, the triangular balcony room is a spectacular private eyrie. The most recent of a long and distinguished line of houses, the Wedge House, like the others, has a matter of fact materials palette. Such houses are direct and robust structures. It is their setting which is sublime.

Israel House. Paradise Beach, NSW. 1986-92.

Each Stutchbury and Pape building is an essay in construction, an explication of how a building is put together, a celebratory description of technique. At one level, this quality is underpinned by Peter Stutchbury's willingness and ability to actually build himself. There is also his intimate knowledge of the functional tradition of the rural shed, born from frequent visits to 'Manuka', his family's property south of Cobar in far west New South Wales. He enjoys the frank formal logic of the rural shed, its direct

STUTCHBURY AND PAPE

adjustment to sun, wind, shade and ventilation. Yet there is also an aspect of expressivity. Stutchbury's buildings, while clear, precise and structurally explicit, appear to have an inner energy, a visually evocative yet tectonically-driven formal expression. The prow-like concrete deck of the Design Faculty Building (1994), announces itself proudly to the undulating bush landscape of the University of Newcastle. On the same campus, the Life Sciences Research Link Building (2001), is a 'horizontal high rise' building of laboratories, offices and teaching spaces. It is a powerfully direct post and beam structure in precast concrete rather than timber. It is as if the lessons of Stutchbury's timber-framed houses have been translated into building for the institution, for designing at

Design Faculty Building. University of Newcastle, NSW. 1994.

a larger scale. To the north, two giant steel props support the massive building as it leaps towards the bush gully beyond. The underbelly is a Herculean space, with diagonal seismic bracing and hanging structural access bridges that evince undeniable visual bombast. Stutchbury also works 'back' from these larger buildings, learning from their technology and experimenting with new formal types. The Liauw House, Seaforth, NSW (2001), is a serene composition of two reinforced concrete framed boxes placed side by side, with gently vaulted ceilings, a cantilevered lap-pool and a double-height gallery. It is an unusual and elegant foray into mass on a steeply sloping treed site overlooking Middle Harbour.

Stutchbury is a 'lyrical technologist'. He invents while he builds. And as he builds, he collects elements that become part of a vocabulary that sings. The Bay House, Watsons Bay, NSW (2001), is a truly beautiful fortified villa, an elaborate expression of formal lyricism matched with a watchmaker's precision. It is a rigorously systematised deployment of detail and syntax, producing what Stutchbury describes as a 'comprehensible tapestry'. With a 600mm module that determines its every line, the Bay House displays an Utzon-inspired fetish for yachting technology, as well as invention in the spirit of architects like John Lautner and Jean Prouvé. The sectional profile of the laminated timber and steel roof truss is a double cantilever, a lyrical metaphor of a bird supporting its wings. At the Cliff House, Newport, NSW (2001), the great cantilevering Cor-ten box beams are an example of structural bravura, they enable the most stunning horizon to be embraced. This is a grand gesture, forthright, like the structural gymnastics of Stan Symonds' 1960s houses on Sydney's North Shore.

The work of Stutchbury and Pape offers a gentle critique, an intelligent reformulation of Jørn Utzon's famous 1962 maxim of 'Platforms and Plateaus' - here applied to the Australian condition. It should read: 'platforms and parasols'. In each of their buildings, the roof literally becomes an umbrella, a technical bird's wing to form a warped or folding surface area which both shades and admits light.

One lives under the parasol, and in many of the houses, there is a further distinction, one sleeps beneath the platform, in the mass of a podium, in the retreat spaces of an analogous rock. Peter Stutchbury designed his first parasol, a tilted plane roof for a church in Port Moresby, Papua-New Guinea (1983), and the motif would reappear in later works. With the Clareville House, NSW (1999), the parasol is a lightweight twisting steel skillion that floats above an almost blank south wall. The podium is a polished concrete slab with bedrooms tucked beneath in a blockwork box. In the Kangaroo Valley Pavilion, NSW (1998), the timber floor becomes a monumental platform. A series of steps running the entire width of the house gives the impression of a temple in the landscape, but the roof, another tilted parasol, appears to take flight.

Kangaroo Valley Pavilion. NSW. 1998.

At the Sydney International Archery Park, Homebush Bay, NSW (1998), a 100 metre long skillion roof twists along its length, and floats above a series of building modules that contain offices, storage and amenities. It is a seemingly endless verandah, the bones of a lean-to shed, and an effortless stroke of line denoting the most fundamental element of shelter - an archetypal sigil of earth (ground) and sky (roof) with the archer as vertical dweller between. With each of these platforms and parasols, no apology is made for the visibility of the vertical support. The roof is no Utzon cloud, but a Stutchbury tree.

The idea of spirit resides in Peter Stutchbury's notion of 'people and places'. The window-seat at the Israel House is a place to rest, and gaze through the trees at the distant dapples of Pittwater. The Bay House has its own crows-nest to escape the world and ponder the horizon. 'Place' on a larger scale in Stutchbury's work means constant partnering with the land. This has much to do with his respect for architects like Richard Leplastrier and Bruce Rickard, and artist Lloyd Rees - who captured the colour, shape and line of Sydney's serpentine shore. The presence of partner and landscape architect, Phoebe Pape, enriches the architecture, makes its gestures ever more ecologically responsible, and above all, subtle.

The spatial, structural and material complexity of Stutchbury and Pape's work defies the myth of 'ease' in the landscape. They realise the archetypal aims of the art of building well, and regain through such building, the promise of memory and paradise.

SYDNEY INTERNATIONAL ARCHERY PARK

STUTCHBURY AND PAPE

north elevation

elevation

elevation

section

plan

SYDNEY INTERNATIONAL ARCHERY PARK | Homebush Bay | NSW | 1998

CLAREVILLE HOUSE

north elevation

north elevation

south elevation

west elevation

upper floor plan

WEDGE HOUSE

east elevation

WEDGE HOUSE | Whale Beach | NSW | 2001

1st floor from south

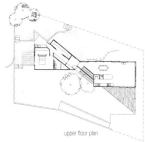

upper floor plan

lower floor plan

east elevation

east elevation

section

WEDGE HOUSE | Whale Beach | NSW | **2001**

NEW DIRECTIONS IN AUSTRALIAN ARCHITECTURE

LIFE SCIENCES BUILDING
THE UNIVERSITY OF NEWCASTLE

north elevation

LIFE SCIENCES RESEARCH LINK BUILDING | The University of Newcastle | NSW | **2001**

in association with Suters Architects

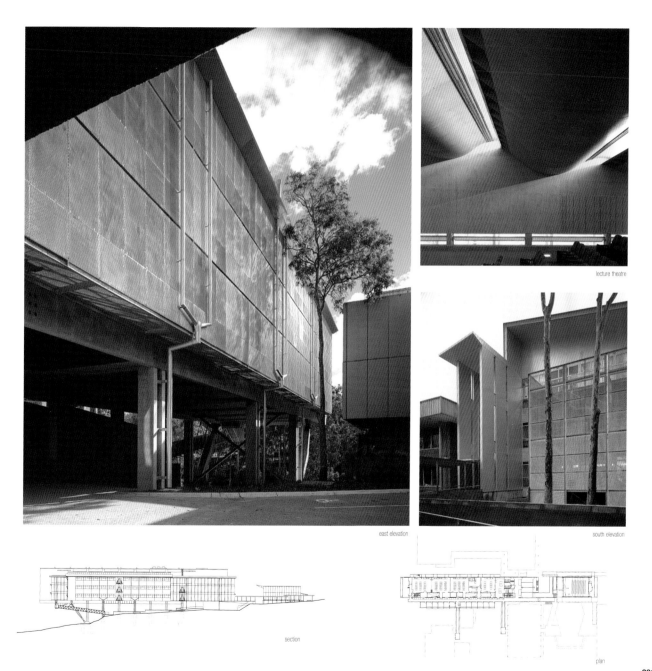

lecture theatre

east elevation

south elevation

section

plan

LIFE SCIENCES RESEARCH LINK BUILDING | The University of Newcastle | NSW | **2001**

NEW DIRECTIONS IN AUSTRALIAN ARCHITECTURE

BAY HOUSE

west elevation

1st floor from east

section

west elevation

east elevation

lower level floor plan

ground floor plan

1st floor plan

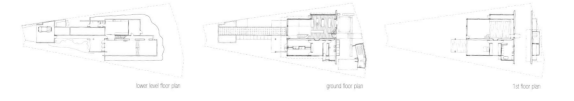

BAY HOUSE | Watsons Bay | NSW | 2001

STUTCHBURY AND PAPE

living space from west

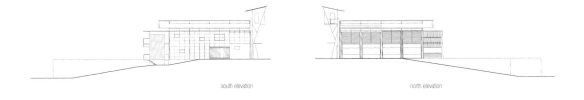

south elevation

north elevation

BAY HOUSE | Watsons Bay | NSW | **2001**

east facade

section

BAY HOUSE | Watsons Bay | NSW | 2001

CLIFF HOUSE

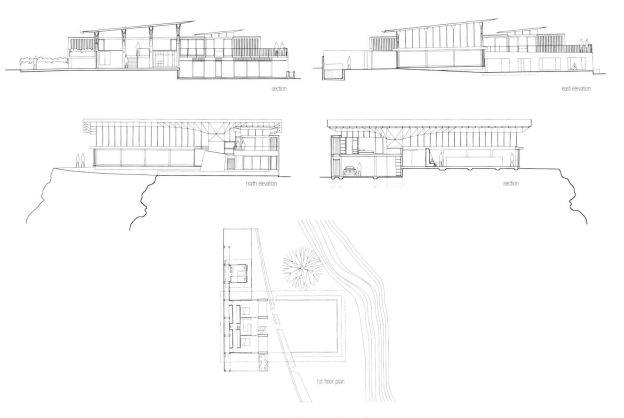

section

east elevation

north elevation

section

1st floor plan

STUTCHBURY AND PAPE

LIAUW HOUSE

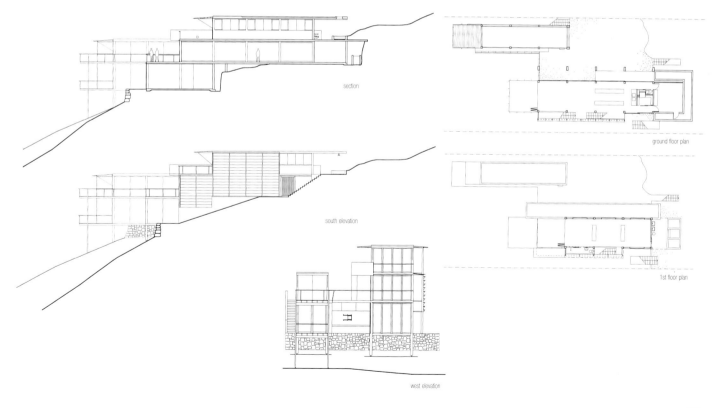

section

ground floor plan

south elevation

1st floor plan

west elevation

KERSTIN THOMPSON

Kerstin Thompson (born Melbourne, 1965) graduated from Royal Melbourne Institute of Technology (RMIT) in 1988. As a student in 1986-87 she worked for MMH Architects, Melbourne and Matteo Thun, Milan. In 1988-89, she worked for Robinson Chen, and in 1990 on site for Perrott Lyon Mathieson at the Telecom Corporate Tower, Melbourne. From 1990 to 1994 she lectured in design at RMIT and worked as a part-time sole practitioner. In 1994 she established Kerstin Thompson Architects Pty Ltd, and in 1998 completed her Masters of Architecture at RMIT. The firm's work has been exhibited in Melbourne, Sydney and Stuttgart. Thompson's buildings have been the subject of numerous articles in journals including *B* (Denmark), *Blueprint* (UK), *Monument*, and *Architecture Australia*. Her writing on 'gradient architectures' was published in *Architecture Australia* (90/3, 2001).

Angelsea House

KERSTIN THOMPSON

Influenced by theorists of landscape architecture and of space, the practice of Kerstin Thompson is committed not only to producing buildings, but to creating new spaces outside of and between buildings. This might seem a simple idea, but it is a response to what Melbourne-based Thompson describes as the forgotten or residual spaces 'that architects are blind to'. Thompson's buildings aim to establish relational space. Dramatic architectural elements, such as walls or an internal drum, become equally important for the spatial relationships they establish. Such gestures are directed less to aesthetic representation than to the experiences of those who dwell in these robust and elegant spaces. Rather than thinking of a building as a mere object, Thompson imagines gradients of spatial experience which establish dialogues between the larger scale of the landscape, the forms of the building, and the consequent intimate haptic spaces.

Working on site in the late 1980s for Ian Robinson and Kai Chen in Melbourne, Thompson acknowledges their influence, especially Chen's, on her early work. The Lorne House (1991), was the start of Thompson's notion of an interior landscape which could be described as a differentiated landscape, bedroom spaces are treated quite dissimilarly to living spaces. An important precedent was Robinson Chen's Hildebrand House, Somers, Victoria (1989-90), with its night-time and daytime mollusc-like volumes. Equally significant was the notion of mass, a requirement resulting from the bushfires that ravaged Victoria's western coastline in 1983. From the beach, the eroded grey stucco forms of the Lorne House witness the larger landscape. At the rear, protected from the southerly winds, is a sun drenched court.

Eighty kilometres away, far above the beach, the Apollo Bay House (1999), is set in the bush with panoramic ocean views. This family holiday house is more literally concerned with the external spaces created by the bending of a thickened wall. Instead of clearing the site or attempting to blend with the landscape, Thompson was intent on letting the form of the house be deformed by its site conditions, and then developing a statement of its own. The result is a house that at one level disappears into the landscape with glazed living volumes and a knife-edge corner, and at another, presents a monumental protective wall as the building hunkers down to meet the winds off Bass Strait.

The strictly limited materials palette of Thompson's work means that her buildings can act as camouflage. The eye is not drawn to symbolic figures. Her buildings are, in her words, simply 'envelopes for living in'. The right gesture is made, then the extra pieces follow. Everything is a consequence of the conscientiously considered 'enabling constraint', as Japanese architect Kazuo Shinohara would have it. Thompson enjoys the initial research and dense assessment of a site and its place, and gleans from that, a key to each design. The James Service Place House, South Melbourne, Victoria (1998), and her Webb Street House, Fitzroy, Victoria (1996), are seamless and silent additions to the close-grained 19th century inner urban landscape of rooftops,

Drum House, Fitzroy, Vic. 2001.

walls and lanes. It is only on close examination that their apparently familiar shapes reveal a subtle play between contextual fit and the disjuncture of the new. The gritty form of the Napier Street Housing, Fitzroy, Victoria (2001), is contextually harmonious, but the eleven apartments, joined together as one elevational picture in brick, read not as 19th century slivers but as a unified landscape wall.

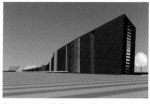

Technology Estate. RMIT University, Bundoora. Vic. (unbuilt)

The Anglesea House (2001), on Victoria's Great Ocean Road, appears to be a departure. Its *sachlich* boxy form and tilt-slab concrete walls go against the idea of the house being deformed by site conditions. Here, an almost suburban site has forced the house to grow vertically, not horizontally. Thompson again makes use of residual spaces, but they are found within a three level prism. The main living spaces are elevated to mid-level to capture views of Point Roadknight, and open onto a double height deck. An external battened stair leads to the roof terrace - this is Le Corbusier's Maison Citrohan by an Australian sea.

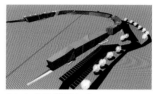

Technology Estate. RMIT University

The effect of Thompson's direct site gestures and interventions reaches a climax in the Drum House, Fitzroy (2001). A glazed drum that acts as a lantern, a 'lung', and internal courtyard has dramatic spatial effect when inserted within the volume of a former sheet metal factory. All the reception, dining, living and study spaces of the house at ground level are the result of this gesture. Unlike Roy Grounds' house, Toorak, Victoria (1953), with a circular court centred in its square plan, Thompson's placement of the drum is deliberately less formal, and is actively dissonant. The result is gracious, and monumental. On the rear façade, existing window openings are sliced vertically, and tall steel French windows with coloured glass have been inserted. Within the drum, perforated timber shades move around, and up and down, their arrangement following the course of the sun as it moves across the cylinder.

In Thompson's larger projects, these themes reappear. With the Hallam Bypass Sound Walls (2001-), both the front and the back of the zig-zagging walls are considered. The reserve on the housing side of the walls becomes usable park space. On the traffic side, an abstract pattern of ochre, charcoal and clear acrylic offers visual stimulus at the drivers' scale. The spaces to either side of the walls are given value. In the 'Long Life, Loose Fit' masterplan proposed for RMIT University's Technology Estate at the Bundoora Campus, there is no fixed functional program, only explicit demands for the adoption of bio-climatic design principles. The building is potentially endless - able to be cut at any point. It has been curved into a huge U-shape, as Thompson says: 'in response to the path of the sun, the building's form and associated skin, articulated by three bands in different degrees of transparency and opacity, twists.' As with all her projects, the directness of such a gesture is confronting, yet matched with disarming humility.

Bypass Sound Walls. Hallam, Vic. 2001-

Bypass Sound Walls. Hallam

LORNE HOUSE

KERSTIN THOMPSON

floor plan

section

LORNE HOUSE | Lorne | Victoria | **1991**

WEBB STREET HOUSE

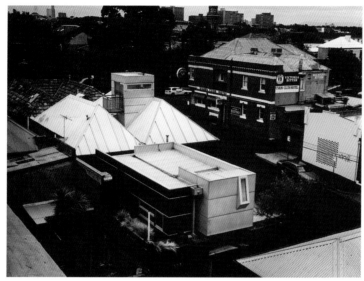

view from south east

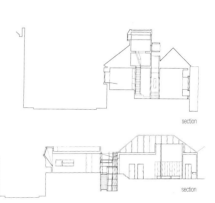

section

section

1st floor plan

view from 1st floor terrace

JAMES SERVICE PLACE HOUSE

KERSTIN THOMPSON

entry from north

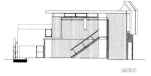

APOLLO BAY HOUSE

KERSTIN THOMPSON

view from north

APOLLO BAY HOUSE | Apollo Bay | Victoria | **1999**

view from south west

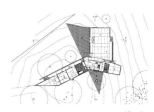

ground floor plan

roof plan

section

view from north east

APOLLO BAY HOUSE | Apollo Bay | Victoria | **1999**

ANGLESEA HOUSE

KERSTIN THOMPSON

east elevation

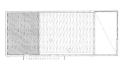

roof plan

1st floor plan

ground floor plan

1st floor looking south east

1st floor looking north

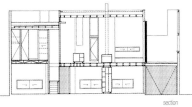

section

west elevation

ANGLESEA HOUSE | Anglesea | Victoria | **2001**

NEW DIRECTIONS IN AUSTRALIAN ARCHITECTURE

NAPIER STREET HOUSING

north elevation

east elevation

north elevation   west elevation   east elevation

DRUM HOUSE

ground floor looking north

DRUM HOUSE | Fitzroy | Victoria | 2001

ground floor looking south

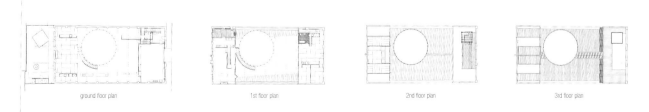

ground floor plan

1st floor plan

2nd floor plan

3rd floor plan

DRUM HOUSE | Fitzroy | Victoria | **2001**

KERSTIN THOMPSON

ground floor

ground floor

1st floor

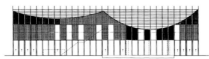

drum elevation

DRUM HOUSE | Fitzroy | Victoria | **2001**

TONKIN
ZULAIKHA
GREER

Peter Tonkin (born Blayney, NSW, 1953) graduated from The University of Sydney in 1977. From 1977-79, he worked for the NSW Government Architect's Office before working for, and collaborating with Lawrence Nield and Partners, then practising independently until 1986. Brian Zulaikha (born Ootacumund, India, 1944) graduated from The University of Sydney in 1967. From 1967-75, Zulaikha travelled and worked in Singapore, Great Britain, Spain and Thailand. While in Sydney, he worked for Allen Jack & Cottier, and Douglas Gordon. From 1975-81, he was a team leader in the NSW Government Architect's Office. From 1981-84, he worked for Wills Denoon before establishing his own practice in 1984. Tim Greer (born 1963, New Zealand) graduated from The University of Auckland in 1988. In 1987, Tonkin joined Zulaikha to form Tonkin Zulaikha, with Tim Greer joining the practice in 1988. Tonkin has taught at University of Sydney, University of NSW, and University of Technology, Sydney. Zulaikha has taught at University of Sydney and University of NSW. The firm's work has been exhibited in Sydney and London. Important completed projects by the firm include: Norton Street Cinema, Leichhardt, NSW (1998); Customs House Refurbishment, Sydney, NSW (1998, with Jackson Teece Chesterman Willis and The City of Sydney); Olympic Plaza Pylons, Homebush Bay, NSW (1999); Australian Pavilion, Expo 2000, Hannover, Germany (2000); Killcare House, Killcare, NSW (2000); and the Challis Avenue Apartments, Potts Point, NSW (2001). The firm's work has been published in numerous books and journals including: *Architectural Review Australia, Architecture Australia; The Architectural Review* (UK); *A+U* (Japan); and *Monument.*

TONKIN ZULAIKHA GREER

Tonkin Zulaikha Greer (TZG) work on the city. As a firm, most of their work has been, and continues to be concerned with public spaces, public buildings, and the rehabilitation of disused industrial and commercial buildings. The politic of the office is brief-oriented: understanding intimately what the program is, and what the existing building or urban context requires. From this comes an assured architectural response that adds another layer, inserts new elements, or knits together a set of urban spaces. The city is understood as a collection of types, fragments, cumulative layers, and successive interventions. The city is perceived as an unfinished project, and as a result, TZG's design work is non-emphatic. This Sydney practice is thus not known for any identifiable formalist signature, yet each intervention is finely honed to the occasion, creating the right measure for shifting the perceptions and preconceptions to another level. For TZG, architecture is about maintaining a constant conversation with the city.

Both Peter Tonkin and Brian Zulaikha have long been involved with sensitive additions and refurbishments of major institutional buildings. In collaboration with Lawrence Nield, Tonkin's competition-winning scheme for the redevelopment of the Overseas Passenger Terminal at Circular Quay, Sydney (1987), led to a highly expressive neo-Constructivist makeover of the 1950s Functionalist buildings on Sydney's waterfront. Zulaikha had been involved in the 1984 restoration of the 19th century façade of Sydney's General Post Office, he and Tonkin had worked together in the NSW Government Architects' Office, and Zulaikha had been design co-ordinator for the entire Circular Quay redevelopment. It was a natural coming together when Tonkin and Zulaikha joined forces in 1987.

Successive projects involving historic buildings and new projects followed. At The Rocks Square, Sydney (1992), a retail centre was developed from a collection of redundant buildings. The Casula Powerhouse, Liverpool, NSW (1995), saw the creation of an arts centre from a disused power station. With the restoration of the Hyde Park Barracks, Sydney (1991), Tonkin Zulaikha provided elegant black steel exhibit cases and stands, in contrast to the hand-rubbed bricks of the original Colonial Georgian building. The reconfiguration of the Customs House, Sydney (1999), in association with Jackson Teece Chesterman Willis and the City of Sydney, saw Tonkin Zulaikha inserting a glazed atrium within the historic building. The sandstone edifice was transformed into a multi-use cultural facility, promoting the city at the very point of traditional

Customs House. Sydney, NSW. 1999.

entry from Circular Quay. The latest TZG scheme following this theme is the redevelopment of a group of wheat silos in Newtown, Sydney (2001-), as an apartment complex. Reinforced concrete silos are appropriated as key urban artefacts, and their distinctive cylindrical volumes become a crucial formal cue. Each of these projects has followed European notions of addition to the city: clever, sensitive, delicate grafts that enliven existing monuments and institutions.

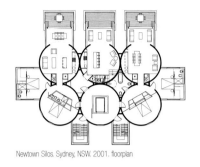

Newtown Silos. Sydney, NSW. 2001. floorplan

Interventions of a more assertive character can be observed in two mixed-use projects by TZG. The Verona in inner Sydney's Paddington, NSW (1995), involved the conversion of an old paper factory into a cinema complex with shops at street level. The final building has no fixed functional image, and its 'natural' fit within the city is achieved as a series of reconfigured fragments. In the Sydney suburb of Leichhardt, TZG transformed a 1970s warehouse into a complex of four cinemas, a restaurant, bar, and bookshop forming the Norton Street Cinema (1998). Public functions are open to the street, there is

Newtown Silos elevation

a broad cantilevering café terrace, and Agit-Prop style signage recalls El Lissitzky - a practical and Productivist art for the people. The aims are not collectivist, but the deployment of intense adjacencies of retail, work and entertainment to encourage a lively urbanity. The Norton St project also marked the emergence of the distinctive design skills of Tim Greer, who became a director in 1997.

The notions of public space, an architecture for the public realm, and architecture as urban furniture, have always been important to TZG. For the Olympic Games held in Sydney, 2000, TZG were commissioned to develop urban design guidelines for the Olympic site at Homebush Bay. The result was an urban design manual that covered paving, lighting, street furniture, and signage. The major physical intervention by TZG was a series of nineteen Olympic Pylons (1999), each 35 metres high, that marched down the 1.6 kilometres of the Olympic Boulevard. These pylons were not intended to be politely urbane street lamps, but dynamic and useful devices that complement the engineering bravado of the sports stadia nearby. Each pylon base is defined as a massive concrete leg supporting a steel tower, and the counter-balancing arm supports a canopy of solar collectors.

Following competition successes, TZG tackled the difficult realm of the monument. In Canberra, ACT, the firm designed the National Memorial to the Australian Vietnam Forces (1992) in association with artist Ken Unsworth, and the Tomb of an Unknown Australian Soldier (1994) with artist Janet Laurence. The Peace Pavilion designed for the Brahma Kumaris Raj Yoga Centre and located in Centennial Park, Sydney, NSW (2000), was a temporary sculptural piece. It had two vertical piers, each visually too heavy for the floating timber platform base, and too robust for the floating timber battened sub-roof above. The pavilion thus suggested the delicate and tenuous balance of human interaction. Emphasised is the unsubtle presence of man negotiating a place for meeting and existence, against the fundamental certainties of earth and sky. A project fraught with issues of representation was the Australian Pavilion for the 2000 World Expo held in Hannover, Germany. TZG's response was a strident and vivid burnt- red pavilion with a floating roof. A 'monumental' lightweight structure, whose openness, mobility and transparency were intrinsically Australian. Here, TZG falter, though not for want of architectural skill - the formality of the pavilion needs a family of like-minded structures so that radical differences from neighbours may be discerned. They needed a city to start to spark their architectural conversation.

The Peace Pavilion. Centennial Park, Sydney, NSW. 2000.

Three residential works indicate TZG's formal diversity, and the application of their office ethic beyond the solely institutional. They continue to emphasise the signature of the process, rather than the creator. A house at Killcare, north of Sydney (2000), designed by Peter Tonkin with Ellen Woolley, is situated on a precipitous slope with a beautiful ocean and beach view. Built of log poles, doubled timber beam construction, clad in fibre cement sheet with a pragmatic skillion roof, the house is unpretentious. It references 1960s Japanese-inspired houses by Allen Jack & Cottier and converses with Sydney's extended coastline 'city' of beach houses as real houses. In complete contrast, a new residence at Lilyfield, NSW (2001-), also by Tonkin and Woolley, is a tough sliver of a house whose brutish side wall is speckled with coloured bricks. This toughness comes from a dialogue with Lilyfield's gritty industrial character, and its proximity to a busy arterial road. At Challis Avenue, Potts Point, NSW, a TZG apartment building (2001), draws its contextual neighbours together into the one building. Two facades (1930s flats on the left, a white painted 1890s house on the right) have been butted together. Copper clad balconies and a copper clad dog-leg facade read as a diagram of function and typological connection. Of the six

Lilyfield House. Sydney, NSW. 2001-.

apartments, four are single level flats while two have double height living volumes resembling stacked *Pavilions L'Esprit Nouveau*. A plate-steel access bridge becomes the bold structural and theatrical gesture within the double height volume. This is the resounding quality of TZG's architecture - maintaining a conversation with a context while providing an appropriate and dynamic stage for human performance. It is an ethic built on respect for the greater realm of the city.

CUSTOMS HOUSE

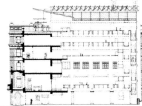

roof plan

ground floor plan

section

CUSTOMS HOUSE | Sydney | NSW | **1999**
in association with Jackson Teece Chesterman Willis and the City of Sydney

PEACE PAVILION

site plan

NORTON STREET CINEMA

TONKIN ZULAIKHA GREER

west elevation

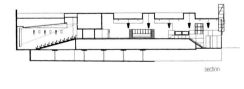

section

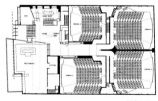

1st floor plan

NORTON STREET CINEMA | Leichhardt | NSW | **1998**

1st floor foyer and entry

NORTON STREET CINEMA | Leichhardt | NSW | **1998**

OLYMPIC PLAZA PYLONS

TONKIN ZULAIKHA GREER

OLYMPIC PLAZA PYLONS | Homebush Bay | NSW | 1999

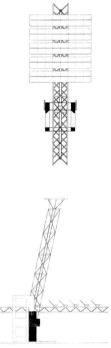

OLYMPIC PLAZA PYLONS | Homebush Bay | NSW | **1999**

AUSTRALIAN PAVILION EXPO HANNOVER 2000

TONKIN ZULAIKHA GREER

photograph © Seewald-Hagen

east elevation

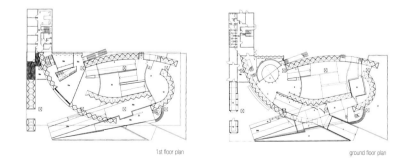

1st floor plan

ground floor plan

AUSTRALIAN PAVILION EXPO HANNOVER 2000 | Hannover | Germany | **2000**

south east corner

north east corner

AUSTRALIAN PAVILION EXPO HANNOVER 2000 | Hannover | Germany | 2000

KILLCARE BEACH HOUSE

TONKIN ZULAIKHA GREER

east elevation

south elevation

north elevation

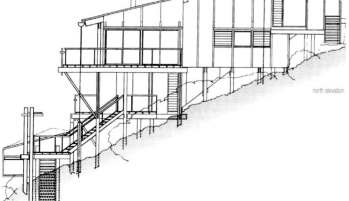

north elevation

stair from west

KILLCARE BEACH HOUSE | Killcare | NSW | **2000**

CHALLIS AVENUE APARTMENTS

south elevation

3rd floor looking north

2nd floor plan

1st floor plan

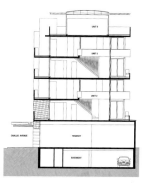

section

CHALLIS AVENUE APARTMENTS | Potts Point | NSW | **2001**

TROPPO

Adrian Welke (born Blyth, SA. 1955) and Phil Harris (born Adelaide, 1956) graduated from The University of Adelaide in 1978. On graduation, Welke worked briefly in Adelaide before moving in 1979 to Darwin, Northern Territory, to work for the Department of Transport and Works, and then for Vin Kenneally and Associates. Harris moved to Darwin in 1979. In 1981, Harris and Welke established the firm of Troppo Architects. In 1993, the Townsville office was opened, and this practice is now run by Geoff Clark. In 1999, Harris returned to Adelaide, opened a branch office, and began teaching at The University of Adelaide. In 2000, a further Troppo office was opened in Perth, run by Fiona Hogg. The firm's work has been exhibited in Paris, Sydney, Melbourne, and Adelaide. Important completed projects include: Low Cost House (Green Can), Karama, NT (1981); Bowali Visitors Centre, Kakadu National Park, Kakadu, NT (1992, with Glenn Murcutt); Pee Wees at the Point, Darwin, NT (1998); Thiel House, Cullen Bay, NT (1998); and Rozak House, Lake Bennett, NT (2001). Welke and Harris self-published their design philosophy in *Punkahs & Pith Helmets: Good Principles of Tropical House Design*, Darwin (1982). The firm's work has been the subject of a monograph, Philip Goad, *Troppo: Architecture for the Top End*, Sydney: Pesaro Architectural Monographs (1999), and has appeared in numerous books and journals including: Jennifer Taylor, *Australian Architecture Since 1960*, Sydney: Law Book Co. (1986); *Casabella* (Italy); *Spazio e Societa* (Italy); *Architecture Australia*; and *The Architectural Review* (UK).

Rozak House

TROPPO

Since 1981, when Adrian Welke and Phil Harris established Troppo Architects in Darwin, an awareness has developed of a unique and regionally specific architectural enterprise in the Top End of Australia. The 'Top End' occupies the northern third of the Northern Territory, it is the area of Australia closest to Indonesia, closer to the equator than Bangkok, and it has a demanding tropical climate with distinctive 'Wet' and 'Dry' seasons. In the past two decades, Troppo have developed ten thematic constants that have not become a restrictive design manifesto, but form a constantly evolving set of general guidelines - part pragmatic and expedient technique, and part phenomenological models. They are deeply felt responses to environment and social behaviour.

The adjustable skin. Troppo's 1980s studies of the building heritage of the Top End revealed the benefits of the adjustable building skin. The example of Beni Burnett's louvred houses, the battens and folding shutters of the early 20th century slatted houses, roll-down blinds, the inventive use of shade cloth, and the laminating of roof eaves like the canopy of a tree all offered simple lessons. The house became an organism of adjustment, its skin like that of humans - an infinitely receptive tissue. One of Troppo's earliest projects was the low cost house prototype nicknamed

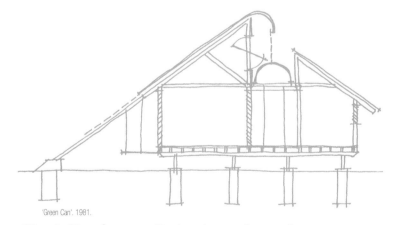

'Green Can'. 1981.

the 'Green Can' (1981), after the signature green Victoria Bitter beer can. Designed around a ventilating breezeway and a roofed outdoor room in the centre of the house, this project was the first in a long series of climatically adjustable houses. The Brieg House, Kununurra, Western Australia (1994), employs a planning principle of external corridors along a verandah, rammed earth walls for a cooling mass, and openings that afford cross-ventilation.

Transported materials. Troppo acknowledge the necessity of imported materials in a place that cannot provide enough natural building materials. The use of corrugated iron, steel framing, plywood timber panels, fibre cement sheet, louvres and the corresponding idea of the building as a prefabricated kit of parts, freely assembled and dissembled, informs their work. The restaurant, Pee Wees at The Point, Darwin, NT (1998), is situated amongst lush tropical trees and palms, and looks across Fannie Bay to

TROPPO

Pee Wees at The Point. Darwin, NT. 1998.

the city. Troppo designed Pee Wees as a transparent skillion roofed pavilion. Glass louvres, translucent polycarbonate and a series of glazed steel doors which fold away to entirely dissolve the south walls, combine with reflective corrugated zincalume on walls, ceilings and soffits to produce an airy succession of terraced spaces. At Pee Wees, Troppo perfected their vision for the non-air-conditioned public space in the tropics, and all with a building palette brought from elsewhere.

'Hearing the Rain'. The thundering of rain in the 'Wet', and the constant dripping of water off broad eaves is part of the Top End. There is no point in escaping from or attempting to block out such natural phenomena. Taking advantage of the elements means, for example, acknowledging the brightness and intensity of the sun in the 'Dry' with its obverse - deep shade. The Top End Hotel, Darwin, NT (1999), is a special place to imbibe. A roofed outdoor bar and a verandah restaurant are separated by pools, decks and landscape gardens that almost invite the rain, and force one to be still, rest, and listen to the downpour on the corrugated roofs.

House as Compound. Troppo plan houses that grow. Guest houses, kitchen decks, and bathrooms can be added as separate entities. The house becomes a community of pavilions with varying degrees of privacy and openness. The multi-level Porcelli-Hazeldine House, Malak, NT is a development of the steel framed treehouse, and it has been growing since 1992. The design was a long-term staged process in which the house would, with separate additions, grow into a compound of pavilions. Dense planting creates the sense of a community of buildings within a private jungle, it also acts as the first filter to the heat and humidity. The latest addition (2001) is the completion of a retreat tower, adding to the studio and guest pavilions. The NHC Aged-Care facility, Pukatja, SA (2000), built for a remote indigenous community is a meandering composition of five sleeping pavilions, a kitchen and a living pavilion. This is the idea of house as compound at a greater scale.

Bali Bathroom. In many Troppo houses, the 'Bali bathroom' becomes a celebration of the act of bathing. Either an open pavilion or open-sided space, it has practical applications, easing problems of condensation and mould in a climate where, at certain times, things never seem to dry. The Thiel House, built on the water at Darwin's Cullen Bay (1998), is inspired by a traditional Balinese courtyard house compound. Designed as a series of five open pavilions, linked by a circulation spine and enclosed gardens space, the Thiel House has a bathroom with one wall totally open to the elements.

While washing, one faces a private landscape and communes with nature.

Nature in the Territory looms larger than man. The landscape and extreme climatic conditions are unavoidable in the Top End. Troppo's architecture responds to the need to keep out the rain and the sun, to reduce heat, and to accommodate humidity. To retreat is pointless. The house is not seen as an impenetrable barrier or fortress, but simply something to live under. Located on a rocky outcrop above Lake Bennett, 80 kilometres south of Darwin, the Rozak House (2001), epitomises a new dynamism in Troppo's response to the land. Three pavilions joined by decks negotiate the rocks and the contours with spidery agility. Two of the roofs are warped corrugated iron "wings", and the third, a skillion, leaps towards the view. In the context of the rugged rocky landscape, gnarled scrub and an overwhelming sky, this house is delicate, almost fragile, a bird temporarily at rest.

The natural chimney. Troppo's buildings avoid the conceit of the flat roof. The gable, or the pyramid roof and its open underside, forms a natural chimney. Even the skillion can

Thiel House. Cullen Bay, Darwin. NT. 1998.

perform a function of drawing air up its sloping length. With roof vents, the building becomes self-ventilating. How to maximise that effect becomes an architectural preoccupation. Troppo's inventive roof forms are not just an aesthetic exercise, but the means to an ecologically sustainable architecture. At the Nganampa Health Clinics, Pukatja, SA (1999), shed roofs are not only economical but practical. The banded wall cladding becomes part of a 'ground' landscape while the roofscape of natural chimneys signs a community of buildings.

The inside-outside house. Catching the breeze becomes a Troppo obsession with the delineation of a perimeter wall. Bringing the battened verandah floor inside the perimeter wall to provide an openly ventilating floor creates an inside-outside house. Troppo have employed these ideas in many of their non-domestic projects for indigenous communities. The huge pyramid of the Marrkolidjban Outstation School, Central Arnhem Land, NT (1992), shades a vast square platform floor creating an internalised verandah, while moveable plywood shutters around the perimeter enable the school to breathe. This same formula, derived from their Tropical House prototype house (1990), was applied to the Gutjangan Outstation School, East Arnhem Land, NT (1993), and the Cone Bay Outstation House, WA (2000), north of Derby.

A house is... For Troppo, a house in many things. In the Top End, in far north Queensland, in remote Western Australia, they find that a house is closer to the idea of a cave or a lightweight aboriginal shelter. Each time one builds, one builds back to those elemental typologies. One virtually camps, builds a house, and 'lives under it'. There is a landing and front steps, small things that increase the house volume to gain intermediary spaces between indoors and outdoors. At Jabiru, NT, as part of a need to provide more rangers' housing for the Kakadu National park, the 'love tents' (1995), one of Troppo's most joyous inventions, are expanded metal-clad and steel framed sleeping boxes elevated above the ground, roofed by stretched paraboloids of white shade cloth, and topped by spherical ventilators. At Berry Springs, in semi-rural savannah, the Kingsley-Khoo House (1997), is an elevated tropical plantation house. Its deep eaves, the sunshades within the gables, the spindly members and transparency also have allusions to traditional timber community houses of Southeast Asia, of a permanent version of Macassan huts. More recent houses such as the Poole House, (2000), Kuranda, in far North Queensland, and the Patteson House, (2001), near Townsville, are dynamic elevated houses with floating skillions that lean forward. A similar expressivity informs the Hay House and the Seaside Apartments at Esperance in Western Australia (1999).

photograph courtesy © Troppo

Poole House. Kuranda, Qld. 2000.

Poole House. Kuranda, Qld. 2000. elevation

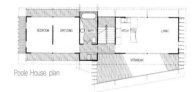

Poole House. plan

The tenth line. Behind all of these strategies is Troppo's notion of the tenth line. When one draws a solid cube, nine lines are required to represent that cube in three dimensions. To draw a tenth line across any of the cube's corners is to immediately imply transparency to the volumetric system. This is an intrinsic design philosophy for Troppo. Their architecture demands the investigation of the open frame and potentially unenclosed volumes. Space is extendible and also infinitely adjustable - if one allows the addition of the tenth line. The Rozak House re-emphasises this idea, but there appears to be the possibility of the tenth line informing the volume of the roof. The warped surface is introduced as the ephemeral but necessary surface of shelter and giver of shade. While the practice celebrates twenty years of existence, it is clear that no end to their experimentation is in sight.

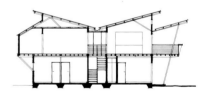

Hay House. Esperance, WA. 1999. section

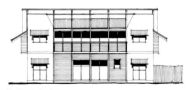

Hay House. elevation

ABORIGINAL COMMUNITY PROJECTS

Wangatha housing, WA. 1999.

Troppo's continuing involvement with Aboriginal communities across Australia is an important component of their practice. Along with several other dedicated practitioners, Troppo have quietly worked to implement a program of ongoing benefit to remote communities. The needs and wants of Aboriginal communities are tangibly different from those presented to conventional architectural practice. The efficacy of the architectural program is underpinned by years of experience, and is built on the research of others committed to this work and the unique challenges provided. 'Housing for Health', published in 1993 by Healthabitat, provided some of the most practical advice on collaborating with aboriginal clients. This publication followed the 'Environmental and Public Health Review within the Anangu Pitjantjatjara Lands' which was carried out in 1986-87. The key issue identified was the direct connection between health and the successful functioning of the house and surrounding living areas. Client involvement with the process was seen as critical.

The sharing of design experience is crucial for architects working in this field. An understanding is required of the cultural issues which determine spatial groupings in the communities, and those who desire proximity to their 'country'. Territoriality and gradations of territoriality can be subtle and nuanced. Prior experience provides the knowledge with which to suggest programs and solutions. Troppo, in all of their work, have focused on the pragmatics of building

Larinyuwar Outstation House. Cone Bay, WA. 2000.

TROPPO

and the economies of structure on a remote site. Obvious problems arise, such as the very fluid nature of the workforce and the limited availability of materials. Serviceability and maintainability determine the choice of materials. No fragile or brittle surfaces can be used - glass is virtually forbidden, for reasons of health, safety, and durability. Most of the houses are metal-framed and metal-clad, termite-proof and easy to transport and replace. The problems of servicing and maintenance have to be dealt with in a realistic way, and a straightforward building system is almost impossible to implement. The circumstances of distance, climatic extremes, and the occasionally less than productive involvement of community children on site are part of the process, and cannot be wished away. The key is to gain from the situation, and to enjoy the real life experience.

Nganampa Health Council, Staff Housing. SA. 1996-

Nganampa Health Council, Health Clinics. SA. 1996-

Kakadu Housing. NT. 1998-2001.

Troppo have brought their concerns with responsible climate control and economical structure to these isolated communities. They have also inevitably provided an element of flair and colour - the architectural signature of Troppo is clearly legible in these remote landscapes. The clinics for the Nganampa Health Council in north-west South Australia (Stage 1 1996-98, and Stage 2 1999-2000) are bright powder-blue pavilions, contrasting with the staff housing clad in yellow and ochre metal sheeting.

Nganampa Health Council, Staff Housing

all photographs on this page courtesy © Troppo

Kakadu Housing, cow-shed

The housing in Kakadu (1998-) references Troppo's earlier work, notably the "Tropical House" of 1990 with its pyramid roof and spherical spinning vent at the apex, here modified and reconfigured as a wall-free pavilion of breezes. Their cow-shed at Kakadu is a low-spreading unpretentious piece of vernacular construction. The forms which have distinguished Troppo's widely publicized architecture in Darwin and the Top End are clearly visible here, stripped down for utility and expedience. The Wangatha housing project (1999), near Laverton, Western Australia, features a series of flying skillion roofs, with walls coloured ochre and green. The Pukatja Aged-Care facility (1999-2000), for the Nganampa Health Council sees a robust and colourful collection of sculpted corrugated-iron blocks linked by curving pathways and shadowed walkways between the buildings. This development is deliberately decentralized, to establish a close relationship with the surrounding country, and to separate the living units of different communities.

The funding for these community projects is usually through the agencies of the Federal Government, such as ATSIC, who then delegate the responsibility to larger regional consultancy organizations. These firms manage the funding, which is often held in trust on behalf of the local community. Although appearing rather paternal, an accountable provision of services and implementation of design quality is ensured. Design and construction consultants then gain work through competitive tender, or by referral.

Troppo realize that the crucial aspect is to listen and look - not to attempt the radical solution. The process is one of exchange and negotiation of ideas. The clients themselves have the local knowledge, and the undeniable fact is that they best understand the land's possibilities and constrictions. The greatest privilege for Troppo is to be continually asked to carry out further work. This indicates that there has been a reciprocal engagement with the community and the process.

Nganampa Health Council, Pukatja Aged-Care Facility. SA. 2000.

Nganampa Health Council, Pukatja Aged-Care Facility

all photographs on this page courtesy © Troppo

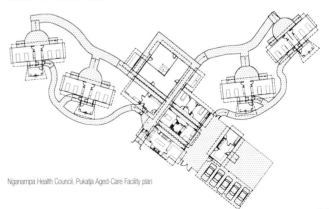

Nganampa Health Council, Pukatja Aged-Care Facility plan

BRIEG HOUSE

view from east

view from north west

BRIEG HOUSE | Kununurra | WA | 1994

P E E W E E S A T T H E P O I N T

south elevation

east elevation

plan

PEE WEES AT THE POINT | Darwin | NT | **1998**

THIEL HOUSE

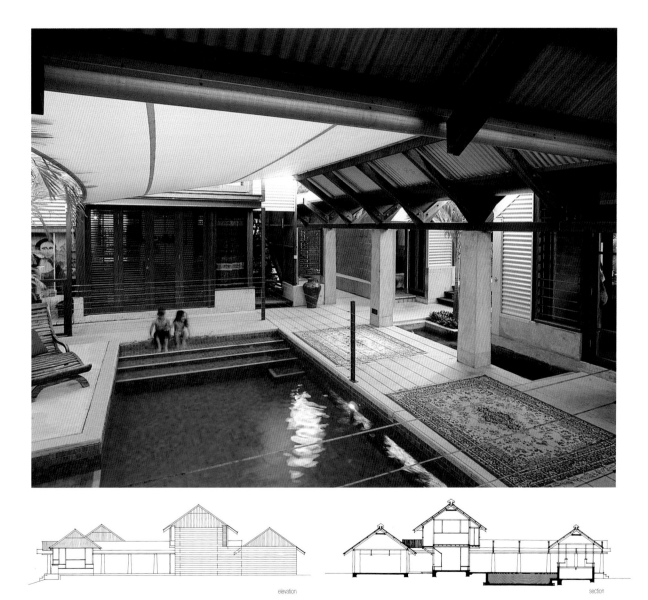

elevation

section

NEW DIRECTIONS IN AUSTRALIAN ARCHITECTURE

TOP END HOTEL

PORCELLI-HAZELDINE HOUSE

view from east

plan

NEW DIRECTIONS IN AUSTRALIAN ARCHITECTURE

ROZAK HOUSE

south elevation

ROZAK HOUSE | Lake Bennett | NT | **2001**

south elevation

ROZAK HOUSE | Lake Bennett | NT | **2001**

TROPPO

north elevation

north walkway

north walkway

kitchen from south

ROZAK HOUSE | Lake Bennett | NT | 2001

JOHN WARDLE

John Wardle (born Geelong, 1956) graduated in architecture from RMIT in 1981. He worked for Cocks and Carmichael, Melbourne from 1982-1986 and established his own practice in mid-1986. He has guest lectured at Columbia University, New York, The University of Western Australia, Adelaide University, The University of Queensland and The University of Melbourne. In 2001, he completed his Masters of Architecture at RMIT University. The firm's work has been exhibited in Stuttgart, Sydney and Melbourne. Important completed projects include Kitamura House, Kew, Victoria (1995); Isaacson Davis House, Balnarring, Victoria (1996); RMIT University Printing Facility, Brunswick, Victoria (2000); Wardle House, Kew, Victoria (2000); and RMIT University Biomedical Laboratories, Bundoora, Victoria (2001). Wardle's buildings have appeared in numerous books and journals including *B* (Denmark), *Wallpaper* (UK), *Monument*, *Architecture Australia*, *UME*, *Architectural Review* (UK) and *Architectural Record* (USA).

Biomedical Laboratories. RMIT, Bundoora

JOHN WARDLE

John Wardle's architecture is driven by the discipline of drawing and detail. He crafts his buildings, first on paper and then on site - where his fascination with joinery details verges on obsession. A process of constant drawing informs both his exquisite joinery pieces and his largest buildings. Each is captured in concrete form by its sectional profile. Wardle's buildings are structures of continuous sectional addition, they are 'cut threads and frayed ends' as he puts it. When spliced together, they reveal 'the character of enclosure'. Wardle learnt much from his experience in the Melbourne office of Cocks and Carmichael. There he learnt the importance of spatial dynamics within a family, and the search for invention through detail. Wardle speaks of that firm's 'ingenious economy', their ability to find proprietary systems, and dispense with half of their operating mechanisms and materials. Wardle's interest in how lines meet in space and in form, how a joint is made, and how in the making of a building any material can be exploited for all of its expressive, structural and sensuous qualities has developed ever since.

After several years of working on house additions, Wardle's first major project was the redevelopment (1989-90) of the Aspendale facilities of the CSIRO. An ability to deal with complex program and service needs was matched with intricate detail and material resolution. The Kitamura House, Kew, Victoria (1995), took that resolve further, with concerns for the designed threshold and the controlled view. Commissioned by a Japanese family living in Australia, this house with a lantern/screen face was designed with the front room as the house's major formal space. Here the tea ceremony is enacted, and the rear of the house was treated as a typically suburban family/living area facing the garden. The house has a Japanese front and an Australian back. The front room is the tallest space in the house, and Japanese only by inference - no *shoji* screens and no *tatami* mats - one could see outside only when seated during the tea ceremony.

On a tea-tree site at Balnarring on the Mornington Peninsula, Wardle made the crucial next step in his development of the open-ended linear container. Built as a weekender, the spaces of the Isaacson Davis House (1996), are arranged in a line with each end represented as a glazed cross-section. To the north, the view is directed down to the native grass and tea-tree landscape, and on the south wall, a dining nook pops out like a fragment of a caravan. Doors slide and unfold, the house can be unpacked, and one leaves the real world and goes on holiday.

The South Yarra House, Victoria (1998), involved the renovation of a large bungalow. Wardle and his clients created the most exquisite series of joinery pieces. Each was a set piece in its own right, containing a story - whether the abstraction of husband and wife as cupboard doors, or as an elaborate

JOHN WARDLE

drawing bench for the children. The house was quilted in battens, shaded and expanded, with the children's bedrooms despatched discreetly to the rear of the site while the 'cut threads' of the main living spaces took priority. A similar hierarchy informs the Portsea Back Beach House (1999). The major living spaces are connected in line, with the minor bedrooms tucked neatly beneath in a blockwork podium. This is no modest 'beach shack' interior, but a generous flaring volume that opens up to the sky and the distant horizon line of Bass Strait. From the south, the house is a glazed timber box floating above the Moonah scrub, while from the north, local granite walls, a seasonal pool and a hall of stairs suggest a monumental entry sequence. Likewise in the farmhouse at Romsey (2000), north-west of Melbourne, the secondary bedrooms are separated into their own 'quarters' while the major living spaces are joined in an arc of timber verticals that continue into the landscape.

If the concerns of these one-off houses indicate formal consistencies, another aspect is the social dimension of Wardle's work for the Salvation Army. On two separate sites in North and West Melbourne (1998-2000), Wardle has designed crisis accommodation centres for single men. Each has been designed in close association with the client. In both cases, Wardle responds directly to the material and formal qualities of site context. Stair volumes gain honorific status, and the dark glazed manganese brick lends distinction with its reference to the bluestone much used in 19th century Melbourne. Seats, canopies, places for meeting, a stair landing, a handrail – with these elements, Wardle is, like the late Aldo van Eyck, conscientious in taking care. It is this same intense attention to the smaller things that characterise his buildings for RMIT University. At the Brunswick campus, the RMIT Printing Facility (2000, in association with Demaine Partnership) constitutes the linking of a series of sectional studies that reflect different lighting, floor loading, and service conditions. The sheer glass curtain wall to Dawson Street acts as a container to house the section - the building is placed in a vitrine. On the building's south-east face, the glazed skin is folded back like a flap to signal entry to a double height corridor. Above, the sectional profile of a brilliant orange marmoleum-clad

Flagstaff Crisis Accommodation Centre. West Melbourne. Vic. 1998-2000

balustrade/seat stretches, extruded, over the entire length of the space. On the building's long west side, Wardle shows how two building parts can be joined together. In the printing process, the notion of registration, or cut of the image, is paramount. At Brunswick, the tilt slabs are in fact mortised together. It is a notion similar to an image found in a favourite book of Wardle's that features Japanese wood block joints. At RMIT University's Bundoora campus, Wardle's Biomedical Laboratories building (2001, in association with DesignInc) is planned about a 160 metre long double-loaded central corridor. To relieve the length, Wardle employs asymmetry at the radial junctions, where natural light is admitted from three light towers that sit above 'event' spaces. Those spaces contain suspended meeting rooms clad in corrugated translucent polycarbonate. Like hanging petri dishes, the amoebic-shaped couches within them appear as cultures in agar. Externally, the spacing of impossibly tall exhaust flues follows its own rhythm. From the prosaic, Wardle has created a symphony of convincing interest.

As his practice takes on work of greater scale and complexity, why does John Wardle continue to design such small elements in large institutional buildings? And why does he expend similar efforts in their realisation in one-off house designs? His own home in suburban Kew (2000) is a climactic summary. There is a linear series of connected major spaces. There is the 'mannered cut' at the street face where the angled slice of façade framed in black plate steel reveals more of the interior. There is the invisibly nailed textured timber cladding where Wardle exhausts the labour component of a cheap material. There are the misaligned curving walls that defer to the root balls and canopies of the adjacent Dutch and Scotch elm trees.

The answer is that Wardle 'sabotages the rational processes of construction.' It is a romantic idea. He designs these elements as pleasures, gifts that might be shared, so that all might touch and experience the most personal outcomes of a designer's hand.

Romsey House. Vic. 2000.

KITAMURA HOUSE

east facade

ground floor plan

KITAMURA HOUSE | Kew | Victoria | **1995**

ISAACSON DAVIS HOUSE

north elevation

floor plan

north elevation

SOUTH YARRA HOUSE

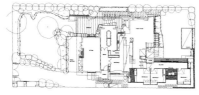

ground floor plan

JOHN WARDLE

SOUTH YARRA HOUSE | South Yarra | Victoria | **1998**

PORTSEA BACK BEACH HOUSE

view from north west

north entry

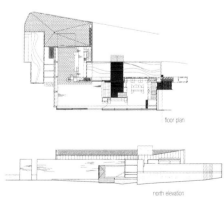

floor plan

north elevation

PRINTING FACILITY RMIT BRUNSWICK

JOHN WARDLE

entry from south east

PRINTING FACILITY | RMIT University | Brunswick | Victoria | **2000**
in association with Demaine Partnership

north elevation

1st floor plan

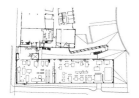

ground floor plan

1st floor corridor

section

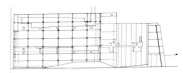

south elevation

north elevation

PRINTING FACILITY | RMIT University | Brunswick | Victoria | **2000**

NEW DIRECTIONS IN AUSTRALIAN ARCHITECTURE

WARDLE HOUSE

south elevation

WARDLE HOUSE | Kew | Victoria | **2000**

entry from south west

1st floor plan

ground floor plan

lower level floor plan

WARDLE HOUSE | Kew | Victoria | **2000**

NEW DIRECTIONS IN AUSTRALIAN ARCHITECTURE

ROMSEY HOUSE

north elevation

view from south west

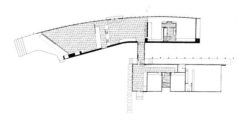

ROMSEY HOUSE | Romsey | Victoria | **2000**

BIOMEDICAL LABORATORIES
RMIT BUNDOORA

JOHN WARDLE

1st floor

BIOMEDICAL LABORATORIES | RMIT University | Bundoora | Victoria | **2001**
in association with DesignInc

east elevation

west elevation

1st floor plan

ground floor plan

BIOMEDICAL LABORATORIES | RMIT University | Bundoora | Victoria | **2001**

WOOD MARSH

Roger Wood (born Melbourne, 1956) and Randal Marsh (born Melbourne, 1958) graduated in architecture from Royal Melbourne Institute of Technology in 1983 and 1991 respectively. After working for several Melbourne architecture practices, they formed Biltmoderne in 1983 with Dale Jones Evans and specialised in architecture, furniture, interior and exhibition design. In 1987, Wood and Marsh established an architectural practice under their own name. The firm's work has been exhibited in New York, London, Frankfurt, Sydney, and Melbourne. Important completed projects include Gottlieb House, Caulfield, Victoria (1994); Stage I Development, Deakin University, Burwood, Victoria (1996); Eastern Freeway Sound Barriers, Doncaster, Victoria (1998); Building 220, RMIT University, Bundoora, Victoria (1998); Bourke Street Footbridge and Gateway, Melbourne, Victoria (1999); Shadowfax Winery and Mansion Hotel, Werribee, Victoria (2001). The firm's work has appeared in numerous books and journal articles including *10x10*, London: Phaidon (2000); Peter Cook et al, *The New Spirit in Architecture*, New York: Rizzoli (1991); *Wallpaper* (UK); *Monument*; *Transition*; *Architectural Review Australia*; and *Architecture Australia*.

Bourke St Footbridge and Gateway

WOOD MARSH

The architecture of Wood Marsh is unashamedly sculptural, and like many works of art, its intent is longevity over expediency. All their buildings veer perilously or oscillate comfortably between serious form-making and sensuous surface. Rather than see these as irreconcilable opposites, Roger Wood and Randal Marsh are content to bring the two together, inviting pleasure rather than angst-ridden puzzle from their emphatically gestural compositions.

As part of the shortlived design firm Biltmoderne (1983-87), Wood and Marsh achieved notoriety for their brazen, almost Warhol-like, search for publicity. Furniture exhibitions, involvement in Melbourne's alternative art and fashion world, and interiors for Inflation (1984), and SubTerrain (1985), nightclubs were ventures into excesses of ornamental surface and formal dynamism, spiced with Wood's abiding interest in structure and composition, and Marsh's acute eye for form and material richness. In a narrow 19th century lane in South Melbourne, their façade for Macrae and Way Studios (1984), was studded with cement roses and a mirrored cartouche, and topped by a cats' ears parapet. In the bush at Eltham, Victoria, the Choong House (1985), was designed as a series of glazed volumes hung off a spine wall of curving limestone. It is a fluid sculptural homage to Heide II at Bulleen by McGlashan and Everist (1968), and a hint of things to come.

In 1987, Wood Marsh established their own architectural firm. They continued to design nightclubs like The Metro (1987), and Chasers, Prahran (1989), but they also decided to focus

Macrae and Way Studios. South Melbourne, Vic. 1984. (as Biltmoderne)

on more permanent work that would lead to wider urban engagement. Conscious efforts were made to revert to a clearer geometry and a restricted materials palette. The Kyritsis House, Eaglemont, Victoria (1988), and the amenities block in Blessington Gardens, St. Kilda, Victoria (1992), were clear indications of this shift in concerns. Yet it was the Gottlieb House in suburban Caulfield, Victoria (1994), that marked an emerging maturity for the partnership.

Unlike the assertive obsession of their Melbourne peers with context and linguistics, Wood Marsh

WOOD MARSH

concentrate on sculptural objects as built form. At the Gottlieb House, a huge elliptical concrete volume punctured by a stainless steel front door faces the street. A textured silver glass box housing the master bedroom's ensuite protrudes above. The contrast of precious metal and austere grey concrete continues inside. The floors, ceilings and pillars in the serene ground level entertaining spaces are treated as a series of textures, from fine to coarse, and in varying tones of grey.

In each Wood Marsh project, the building footprint holds the crucial gestural germ of a sculptural project. At the Burwood campus of Deakin University, Wood Marsh in association with Pels Innes Neilson and Kosloff (PINK) designed a series of five dynamically sited buildings (1996), each with its own distinctive external skin, spinning off in plan around a corkscrew stair. Building C acts as a seven storey signpost for the campus, with curving walls of polished white precast concrete punched with tall slim window openings. Building G has a folded exposed aggregate wall hovering above a ground level cloister space,

while Buildings D, E, and F adopt a common language for their skins - a tapestry of mild steel plates sitting proud on a glazed skin wall. Black, deep charcoal grey, silver and white make up the colour palette, and smooth and polished, rough and etched, sticks and mirrors form the texture palette. A later work, Building J (1998), introduces another texture, concrete as corduroy patchwork. The building's long west façade is given three dramatic and discrete surface treatments, an ironic billboard of public art giving the illusion of three buildings instead of one.

At RMIT University's Bundoora campus, Wood Marsh (again with PINK) introduce a bold textural and planning concept to an unremarkable outer suburban campus. Their Building 220 (1998), is a brilliant terra cotta curving 'bridge' between rusticated abutments, A & G Curtis House. Richmond, Vic. 2000.
providing an emphatic counterpoint to the twisted trunks of the ancient red gums. The arc reads as a metallic fusilage, while in an ironic twist, the rock textured concrete abutments are perforated with circular windows. These university buildings are formal reflections on texture, tectonics, and colour as expressed through a building's skin.

Wood Marsh's work also includes large scale works of urban design. The Eastern Freeway Sound Barriers (1996, in association with PINK) run for ten kilometres through the Melbourne suburbs. Wood Marsh treat infrastructure as a giant piece of Land Art. Textured concrete walls in black, white and grey run in great overlapping swathes, softened and offset by carefully chosen tones of native grasses. The same approach to urban design as public art informs Wood Marsh's design for the Bourke Street Footbridge and Gateway (1999), to the Melbourne Docklands. With a nod to artist Jenny Holzer, the two monumental pylons facing the end of Bourke Street have bands of red neon marching constantly up their length, while pedestrian ramps zig-zag up and through each pylon. On the bridge itself, erect red shafts curve upward in quizzical salute and become fluorescent tube lights.

Wood Marsh extend their seductive repertoire in the Taylor House, Prahran, Victoria (1999). Black is the dominant colour in this vast loft-like house built on top of a suburban warehouse. The surprises are a Barbarella-style TV 'womb', and a blood-red swimming pool in the rooftop courtyard. In Richmond, two townhouses, each with a square plan over three levels, are given dramatically different treatment. The S & H Curtis House (1999), with its white gallery-like interiors, has a north-facing summit of deep white fins that enclose a stunning glass stair. The A & G Curtis House (2000), has a Missoni jumper façade

Prince of Wales Hotel, St Kilda, Vic. 2001.

knitted in slivers of slim grey, black and white concrete bricks, punctuated with boxed metal window frames. On the top floor, a perforated stair terminates at a Manhattan-style volume, and windows punched in the walls strategically picture Melbourne landmarks. Above the 1930s Moderne styled Prince of Wales Hotel, St Kilda, Victoria, Wood Marsh's addition of a rooftop bar and spa (2001), is treated as a formation of rusted steel fins framing a series of timber-filigree screens, creating a weathered L-shaped crest on the skyline.

Bringing together these themes of abstract modern sculpture and sensuous surface are two projects on one site: the Mansion Hotel and Shadowfax Winery at Werribee Park, 30 kilometres west of Melbourne. The hotel comprises additions to and refurbishment of the former St Joseph's Seminary (1923). Deferring to the dour classicism of the original building, Wood Marsh added an urbanely black, white and grey residential and recreation wing, its monumentality echoing the 1960s neoclassicism of Philip Johnson and his Melbourne acolyte Guilford Bell. A short walk away is the Shadowfax Winery, a striking piece of abstract formalism that is appropriately rude in its agrarian robustness, yet simultaneously mysterious. Four wedge shaped volumes house the prosaic linear function of winemaking, and are clad in rusted Cor-Ten steel. Like Paul Virilio's abject fascination with the concrete bunkers of France's Atlantic coast, this is an aestheticization of the monolith. Like so many of Wood Marsh's buildings, the Shadowfax Winery tenders three intrinsic qualities: aspirations to Land Art, gorgeous materiality, and the patina of silent age. These buildings are not so much concerned with climate or structure, as with sensual and formal reverie.

NEW DIRECTIONS IN AUSTRALIAN ARCHITECTURE

ST KILDA AMENITIES BLOCK

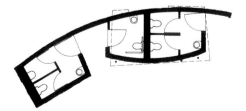

ST KILDA AMENITIES BLOCK | St Kilda | Victoria | **1992**

GOTTLIEB HOUSE

west elevation

ground floor

GOTTLIEB HOUSE | Caulfield | Victoria | **1994**

WOOD MARSH

BUILDING 220 RMIT BUNDOORA

west elevation

BUILDING 220 | RMIT Bundoora | Victoria | **1998**
in association with Pels Innes Neilson and Kosloff (PINK)

east elevation

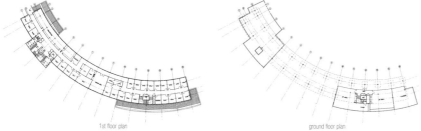

1st floor plan

ground floor plan

BUILDING 220 | RMIT Bundoora | Victoria | **1998**

BUILDINGS C-G DEAKIN UNIVERSITY

WOOD MARSH

1st floor view from north to building F

BUILDINGS C-G | Deakin University | Burwood | Victoria | **1996**

in association with Pels Innes Neilson and Kosloff (PINK)

view from north to building C

BUILDINGS C-G | Deakin University | Burwood | Victoria | **1996**

NEW DIRECTIONS IN AUSTRALIAN ARCHITECTURE

view from south

BUILDINGS C-G | Deakin University | Burwood | Victoria | **1996**

view from east

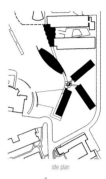

site plan

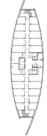

building C floor plan

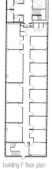

building F floor plan

BUILDINGS C-G | Deakin University | Burwood | Victoria | **1996**

WOOD MARSH

EASTERN FREEWAY SOUND BARRIERS

EASTERN FREEWAY SOUND BARRIERS | Doncaster | Victoria | **1998**

in association with Pels Innes Neilson and Kosloff (PINK)

BUILDING J DEAKIN UNIVERSITY

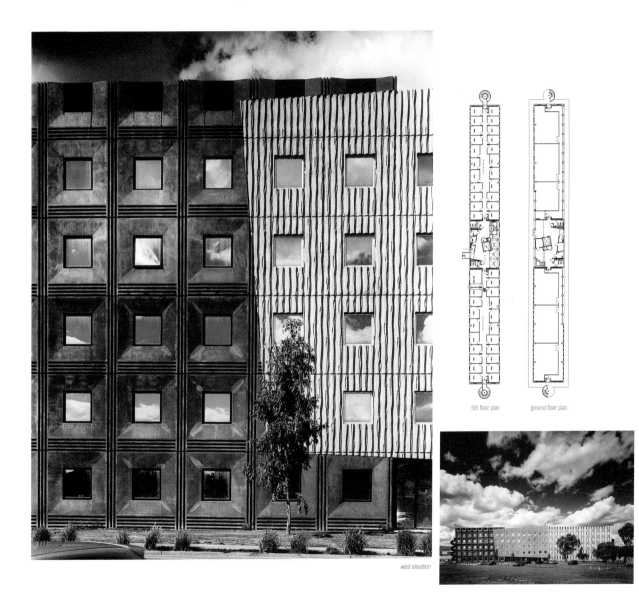

5th floor plan   ground floor plan

west elevation

BUILDING J | Deakin University | Burwood | Victoria | **1998**
in association with Pels Innes Neilson and Kosloff (PINK)

289
/projects

NEW DIRECTIONS IN AUSTRALIAN ARCHITECTURE

S & H   C U R T I S   H O U S E

2nd floor

ground floor plan   1st floor plan   2nd floor plan

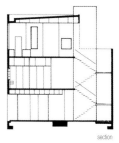

section

S & H CURTIS HOUSE | Richmond | Victoria | **1999**

TAYLOR HOUSE

floor plan

TAYLOR HOUSE | Prahran | Victoria | **1999**

THE MANSION HOTEL

east elevation

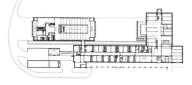

ground floor plan

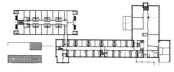

1st floor plan

cross section St Joseph's wing

view from north east

SHADOWFAX WINERY

north elevation

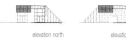

section

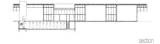

elevation north   elevation south

ground floor plan

roof plan

east elevation

SHADOWFAX WINERY | Werribee | Victoria | **2001**

BOURKE STREET FOOTBRIDGE AND GATEWAY

WOOD MARSH

view from west

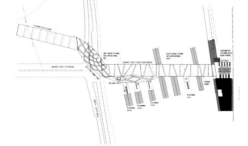

BOURKE STREET FOOTBRIDGE AND GATEWAY | Melbourne | Victoria | **1999**

Published by Periplus Editions, with
editorial offices at 130 Joo Seng Road
#06-01, Singapore 368357.

Editor: Patrick Bingham-Hall
Design: Jodi Anderson Design
Photography © 2005 Patrick Bingham-
Hall except where otherwise credited.
Text © 2005 Philip Goad
and Pesaro Publishing

Published by arrangement with
Pesaro Publishing, Sydney, Australia.

ISBN 0-7946-0337-8

Distributors

North America, Latin America & Europe
Tuttle Publishing
364 Innovation Drive
North Clarendon, VT 05759-9436
Tel: (802) 773 8930
Fax: (802) 773 6993
Email: info@tuttlepublishing.com
www.tuttlepublishing.com

Japan
Tuttle Publishing, Yaekari Building, 3F,
5-4-12 Osaki, Shinagawa-ku;
Tokyo 141-0032.
Tel: (03) 5437 0171;
Fax: (03) 5437 0755
E-mail: tuttle-sales@gol.com

Asia Pacific
Berkeley Books Pte Ltd
130 Joo Seng Road #06-01/03,
Singapore 368357.
Tel: (65) 6280 1330;
Fax: (65) 6280 6290
E-mail: inquiries@periplus.com.sg
www.periplus.com

Printed in Singapore

09 08 07 06 05
5 4 3 2 1